# Pyrrhonism

# Studies in Comparative Philosophy and Religion

**Series Editor: Douglas Allen, University of Maine**

This series explores important intersections within and between the disciplines of religious studies and philosophy. These original studies will emphasize, in particular, aspects of contemporary and classical Asian philosophy and its relationship to Western thought. We welcome a wide variety of manuscript submissions, especially works exhibiting highly focused research and theoretical innovation.

*Varieties of Ethical Reflection: New Directions for Ethics in a Global Context*, by Michael Barnhart

*Mysticism and Morality: A New Look at Old Questions*, by Richard H. Jones

*Gandhi's Experiments with Truth: Essential Writings by and about Mahatma Gandhi*, by Richard L. Johnson

*To Broaden the Way: A Confucian–Jewish Dialogue*, by Galia Patt-Shamir

*Pyrrhonism: How the Ancient Greeks Reinvented Buddhism*, by Adrian Kuzminski

*Ethics of Compassion: Bridging Ethical Theory and Religious Moral Discourse*, by Richard Reilly

# Pyrrhonism

## How the Ancient Greeks Reinvented Buddhism

Adrian Kuzminski

LEXINGTON BOOKS

A division of
ROWMAN & LITTLEFIELD PUBLISHERS, INC.
*Lanham • Boulder • New York • Toronto • Plymouth, UK*

LEXINGTON BOOKS

A division of Rowman & Littlefield Publishers, Inc.
A wholly owned subsidary of The Rowman & Littlefield Publishing Group, Inc.
4501 Forbes Boulevard, Suite 200
Lanham, MD 20706

Estover Road
Plymouth PL6 7PY
United Kingdom

Copyright © 2008 by Lexington Books
First paperback edition 2010

*All rights reserved.* No part of this publication may be reproduced,
stored in a retrieval system, or transmitted in any form or by any
means, electronic, mechanical, photocopying, recording, or otherwise,
without the prior permission of the publisher.

British Library Cataloguing in Publication Information Available

**Library of Congress Cataloging-in-Publication Data**
Kuzminski, Adrian, 1944–
  Pyrrhonism : how the ancient Greeks reinvented Buddhism /
Adrian Kuzminski.
        p. cm. — (Studies in comparative philosophy and religion)
  Includes bibliographical references.
  1.  Pyrrhon, of Elis—Influence.  2.  Buddhism.  I. Title.  B613.K89 2008
    186'.1—dc22                                        2008010723

ISBN: 978-0-7391-2506-9 (cloth : alk. paper)
ISBN: 978-0-7391-2507-6 (pbk : alk. paper)
ISBN: 978-0-7391-3139-8 (electronic)

Printed in the United States of America

∞™ The paper used in this publication meets the minimum requirements of
American National Standard for Information Sciences—Permanence of Paper
for Printed Library Materials, ANSI/NISO Z39.48–1992.

To the memory of Everard Flintoff

# Contents

# Preface

Pyrrhonism is commonly confused with scepticism in Western philosophy. But unlike sceptics, who believe there are no true beliefs, Pyrrhonists suspend judgment about *all* beliefs, including the belief that there are no true beliefs. Pyrrhonism was developed by a line of ancient Greek philosophers, from its founder Pyrrho of Elis in the fourth century BCE through Sextus Empiricus in the second century CE. Pyrrhonists offer no view, theory, or knowledge about the world, but recommend instead a practice, a distinct way of life, designed to suspend beliefs and ease suffering. Since beliefs are attachments to what is nonevident, they say, and are therefore distorting, uncertain, and subject to challenge and contradiction, they generate anxiety and fear, compounding suffering. By suspending judgment on beliefs, Pyrrhonists seek to liberate themselves from attachment to things nonevident; having achieved this, they claim a certain tranquility (*ataraxia*) follows. Only appearances are evident, they say, these being sensations and thoughts which we cannot help having, which are involuntary, and it is by them rather than by our beliefs that we should live.

Pyrrhonism bears a striking similarity to some Eastern non-dogmatic soteriological traditions, particularly Madhyamaka Buddhism. Indeed, its origin can plausibly be traced to the contacts between Pyrrho and the sages he encountered in India, where he traveled with Alexander the Great. Even though Pyrrhonism went on to develop in a Greek idiom without reference to Eastern traditions, the similarity of views is remarkable, suggesting a commonality of insight not much explored. Although Pyrrhonism has not been practiced in the West since ancient times, its insights occasionally have been independently recovered, most recently in the work of Ludwig Wittgenstein. They remain relevant, perhaps more than ever, as an antidote to today's cultures of belief.

—◡◡◡—

I think of this book as growing out of two trips, one to a series of ancient Greek sites in Italy, Greece, and Turkey in 1994, and the other to Benares, India, in 2001. The tactile reality of these places gave some kind of flesh to years of thinking and reading in Western philosophy and, increasingly, in Asian traditions of liberation. My interest in Asian thought and culture was sparked earlier by a decade of teaching at the University of Hawaii back in the 1970s, where Asian specialists predominated in most fields, including my own history department. For me, trained as a specialist in European intellectual history, my Hawaiian experience was a healthy corrective to the Eurocentrism of my previous education.

After leaving Hawaii and settling in rural upstate New York, I wrote a book, *The Soul*, in 1994, which took the Wittgensteinian tactic of trying to separate what can be said from what can be shown and applied it to George Berkeley's distinction between perceptions and the perceivers of those perceptions. In subsequent years I continued to find parallels between this approach and South Asian philosophical and religious traditions, especially Buddhism, and particularly the Madhyamaka. Like Wittgenstein and Berkeley, Buddhists emphasized not knowledge but liberation from suffering, and like them they did so in a context that distinguishes between the objects of consciousness and consciousness itself. And always in the back of my mind were the Pyrrhonists of the ancient Greco-Roman West, who had intrigued me since graduate school, and who I believed pursued a similar path.

What began to bring these threads together was a reading of Everard Flintoff's 1980 article in *Phronesis* entitled "Pyrrho and India." Flintoff, like others before him, saw a connection between ancient Greek Pyrrhonism and early Buddhism, a connection suggested by Pyrrho's trip to India with Alexander the Great. But he took it more seriously and offered, as a sketch, the beginnings of a systematic comparison between Buddhism and Pyrrhonism. I thought a closer comparison of classical Buddhist and Pyrrhonian texts beyond what Flintoff presented was warranted, and the result was a paper, "Pyrrhonism and the Madhyamaka," published in *Philosophy East and West* in October 2007, most of which is incorporated in the second chapter of this work. I then saw that the affinity between Pyrrhonism and Buddhism had larger implications, and the result is this book.

I would like to thank above all C. W. Huntington, Jr., my friend and colleague at Hartwick College and author of *The Emptiness Of Emptiness*. It was with "Sandy" (Professor Huntington) that I traveled to Benares, along with a group of students, in 2001. He has been unfailingly enthusiastic and extraordinarily helpful with this project, bringing his expertise to bear on the major issues at hand, as well as providing technical assistance with Sanskrit terminology. Without him this book would never have been written. Its shortcomings, of course, must be mine alone to bear. I also owe a great debt to my friend the art historian Keith Harrington. It was with Keith that I visited nearly fifty ancient Greek sites scattered across the Mediterranean world. The ruins of mostly sacred architecture reminded me that ancient Greek culture was more steeped in soteriological concerns that we normally assume. I am also indebted to Professor Stanley Konecky of the philosophy department at Hartwick College, who made it possible for me to pursue my research for this book and other projects as resident scholar in philosophy, beginning in 1997. I also benefited very much from yearly lectures I gave at the college, many of them on aspects of this work, and from my students there, particularly those in a recent course on scepticism. I am grateful as well to the editors of *Philosophy East and West*, and the anonymous readers there, who helped me hone my arguments in comparative philosophy.

# Foreword

## C. W. Huntington, Jr.

This is a work of comparative philosophy. As such, it inserts itself between two disparate academic camps, each with a very real claim on the intriguing terrain staked out by Dr. Kuzminski. On the one side there are the philologists and historians who specialize in ancient Greek philosophy. On the other are the Indologists, whose area of expertise encompasses the literature of early Indian Buddhism. No doubt both groups will find reasons to criticize this book. Given the notorious difficulties of any genuinely comparative endeavor, one must ask: What are the justifications for undertaking such a task? And what are its potential rewards?

The justification for any serious work of comparative scholarship is, by definition, that it invites us to leave behind the familiar domain governed by specialists of every stamp and enter into disputed territory. This is precisely why comparative studies like this one are risky and vulnerable to criticism from a number of quarters. However, in going where the specialists themselves are unwilling or ill-equipped to go, we stand the chance of discovering some new, unanticipated perspective on matters previously thought to be settled. In this case, we may come away, first of all, with a new understanding of Pyrrhonism.

Kuzminski argues that Pyrrho's teaching has been severely distorted by his interpreters, both ancient and modern. Specifically, since ancient times commentators have failed to appreciate what it means truly to suspend judgment on nonevident matters, as Pyrrho claimed to do. They have also misconstrued Pyrrho's insistence on the necessity of affirming the appearance of the world as nothing more, or less, than appearance. Consequently, Kuzminski concludes, Pyrrho has been mistakenly interpreted as offering a philosophical theory or view, rather than as suggesting a soteriological practice—a practical means of liberation from the anxiety generated by clinging to beliefs of any kind.

In order to allow us to see Pyrrho through a new lens, Kuzminski has to pry his work from the hands of the acknowledged authorities. According to the received interpretation of Pyrrho, he is one of the sceptics. More, beginning with the recovery of Pyrrhonian texts in the Renaissance, we have been told—and up to now, we have had little reason to doubt—that Pyrrho represents the most extreme form of scepticism. In this way his work has been comfortably inserted into the canon of European philosophy; today it is commonly read as a bit of marginalia, an ancient Greek school with little or nothing of interest to say to modern philosophers. All of these assumptions can now be revisited.

We know that Pyrrho journeyed to India, along with Alexander the Great, in the fourth century BCE. According to Diogenes Laertius, it was there, in conversation with Indian sages, that he worked out the rudiments of his "most noble philosophy." Kuzminski carefully examines the historical evidence supporting this tradition. And so it happens that, in reading this book, we stand to gain a more nuanced understanding not only of Pyrrhonism, but of Buddhism as well.

Of all the apparent conundrums of Indian Buddhism, none is more vexing than Nāgārjuna's insistence that he holds no philosophical theory or view. Since at least the fifth century in India, with the work of the doxologist Bhāvaviveka, this claim (if indeed that is what it is) has been compromised by attempts to secure a place for Nāgārjuna in the philosophical canon. In order to do so, Nāgārjuna's writing has had to be interpreted as the exposition of a theoretical position, rather than as a medicine for curing the suffering caused by clinging. Ironically, in this respect Nāgārjuna's fate in India mirrors that of Pyrrho in Europe. However, in skillfully juxtaposing these two philosophers—as Kuzminski does here—early Indian Madhyamaka is released from centuries of cumbersome scholasticism and speaks to us with a startlingly fresh and original voice.

The distinct possibility that there are historical as well as philosophical connections between Pyrrhonism and Buddhism provides a fascinating backdrop to the ideas presented here. This is a courageous and edifying piece of scholarship, the kind of book that would most likely never be written by a specialist in either Greek or South Asian philosophy.

# Why Pyrrhonism is
# Not Scepticism

Pyrrhonism is an unusual ancient Western philosophy. An active tradition in antiquity, it has since lain dormant, with rare exception. It
constitutes a novel approach to human experience, one which may
prove useful in our troubled times. It is not, like the other ancient
Western philosophies, a view or theory or belief of any sort. Rather it
is a practice, a distinct way of life, developed by a line of ancient Greek
philosophers, beginning with Pyrrho of Elis at the end of the fourth
century BCE, and continuing through Sextus Empiricus, a Greek
physician who lived in the second century CE whose surviving texts
are the principal Pyrrhonist writings we have. These philosophers
were unique in the West in consciously *not* developing beliefs about
nonevident matters, pro or con. Such beliefs, they maintained, being
about things nonevident, could not be substantiated, and so remained
unstable and open to challenge from competing beliefs. Their instability meant those beliefs could not be embraced with certainty, and this
lack of certainty, along with its consequences (concern, anxiety, fear,
etc.), was a principal source of human suffering, according to the
Pyrrhonists. Beliefs about things nonevident therefore were to be
avoided, they recommended, and their philosophy addressed how this
might be achieved.

Pyrrhonists, however, did accept the testimony of what is evident,
that is, of the immediate, involuntary experiences we have of sensations and thoughts, and they accepted reliable inferences from these to
other immediate involuntary experiences of sensations and thoughts
we are likely to have in the future. These kinds of inferences, as Sextus Empiricus put it, "are found convincing by everyday life: seeing
smoke, someone diagnoses fire; having observed a scar, he says that a

wound was inflicted,"[1] and so on. Beyond this, however, they saw no need to go, and harm in the prospect. They advocated instead ceasing or suspending (*epochē*) judgment about claims beyond present or possible immediate experiences. Once such judgments were suspended, they found that a certain liberation from anxiety followed, at least with regard to the uncertainties posed by the beliefs in question, bringing peace of mind and openness. Pyrrhonists called this liberation from anxiety *ataraxia*, originally a military term indicating calm by soldiers under attack. The term is negatively put since it is a freedom *from* distraction, confusion, ignorance, disorder, panic, etc., rather than the achievement of some kind of particular positive state. With *ataraxia*, appearances, no longer confused with the distracting and confining beliefs ordinarily held about them, could now be appreciated for what they were, thus opening the way to a new, nondogmatic way of life. This philosophy—developed in ancient Greece but apparently inspired by contacts with India—is the subject of this book.

In spite of its unique and interesting stance towards experience, and perhaps in part because of it, philosophers and scholars of philosophy have largely overlooked Pyrrhonism. Although it has received some serious attention over the years, no systematic work on the subject exists in the English language as far as this writer can determine, an omission this book hopes to help rectify. I shall argue that the place Pyrrhonism has been given in the tradition of Western philosophy has largely retarded rather than advanced our understanding of it. It did not survive antiquity as a way of life even though it was rediscovered in the early modern era, first with the circulation in the fifteenth century of the manuscripts of the works of its principal surviving author, Sextus Empiricus, and later with the publication Latin translations of Sextus' works in Paris in 1562 and 1569.[2] In spite of this, Pyrrhonism has rarely been taken seriously in modern times on its most basic terms: as a therapeutic and liberating practice advocating no views. There have been, however, as we shall see, some interesting modern reinventions of the ancient philosophy. But, on the whole, dogmatists of one school or another have mined its texts in modern times for arguments to use against their equally dogmatic opponents. More significantly, both in antiquity and more recently, Pyrrhonism has consistently been confused with its philosophical rival, scepticism, and it is this confusion more than any other that has dogged any deeper understanding and appreciation of Pyrrhonism.

In considering Pyrrhonism as a wholly separate tradition, this work aims to dispel the confusion between it and what is normally understood by scepticism. It is true that Pyrrhonists called themselves sceptics, among other things, but they did so only in the original Greek sense of the word, *skeptikos*—a seeker, one who enquires or examines, considers, deliberates, etc.[3] Furthermore, unlike what the word "sceptic" later came to mean, they questioned not all assertions, but only those made concerning nonevident matters. The Pyrrhonists' aim, unlike that of subsequent sceptics, was not to doubt or undermine such knowledge claims, but to see whether or not they could be determined, that is, confirmed, by self-evident experience. Absent such a confirmation, they did not deny such claims, but instead suspended judgment about them. According to Pyrrhonists, beliefs about evident experience can be confirmed or disconfirmed only by some subsequent evident experience. The sun will or will not rise tomorrow morning, and we speak loosely about "believing" it will do so. We can believe the sun will rise tomorrow, but need not do so; we can expect it without having to believe it on reliable probability. Beliefs, as I will use the term, are assertions about things not temporarily but persistently nonevident. If a belief becomes evident, it becomes a fact or appearance rather than a belief. Beliefs about persistently nonevident matters—that the sun, say, is the god Apollo—can neither be confirmed nor disconfirmed, as Pyrrhonists point out. They remain beliefs.

The term scepticism early on shifted from an emphasis on doubt as a tool of enquiry to doubt as an end in itself, calling enquiry itself into question. To doubt a nonevident belief is to raise some objection that contradicts or otherwise undermines that belief. A sceptic, already in antiquity, as we shall see, came to mean primarily someone prone not only to doubt nonevident claims about experience, but also to take such doubts as evidence of the falsity of those beliefs rather than of the inconclusiveness of the enquiry. Scepticism, originally born out of the impulse to sort out the evident from the nonevident, by Hellenistic times had acquired a distinctly negative stance; it itself became, ironically, a belief in something nonevident, namely that an objection to a judgment is itself a reason to refute rather than suspend it. Once this new and curious belief became established—as it was in Plato's Academy by the middle of the third century BCE—it was soon turned against evident as well as nonevident things; objections to beliefs about evident things were taken to call into question even what is evident. Once made dogmatic in this way, scepticism knew no bounds.

Sceptics ancient and modern, unlike Pyrrhonists, question evident things as well as those nonevident, claiming that our senses deceive us, as when we see an oar bent in water but straight to the touch. They jump to the paradoxical conclusion that direct experience (in this example, the visual and tactile experiences of the oar in and out of water) is somehow nonevident. Our sensory experience, they argue, is only apparently evident; in reality, they say, it is illusory and unreliable. In drawing this conclusion, they confuse, according to Pyrrhonists, direct experience with belief about direct experience. Pyrrhonists also discuss such anomalies of direct experience as the oar straight and bent, but they find in them no evidence to discredit our senses or thoughts; the problem, they say, arises instead from various dogmatic judgments made *about* our experience, such as the assumption that our senses are internal representations of external objects. The oar bent in water anomaly does not suggest there is anything wrong with our senses of vision and touch, which in fact display what they display reliably and evidently; it rather suggests, according to Pyrrhonists, that there is something wrong with the assumption that some kind of hidden but consistent substance underlies such phenomena. It is the latter the anomaly calls into question, not the former.

Non-Pyrrhonian sceptics, Pyrrhonists maintain, go too far in making doubt absolute and indiscriminate, in making the denial of everything inevitable. Confident of not allowing any positive assertions to be made, they draw the negative conclusion that no positive assertions can ever be made, and that even what is apparent must somehow be an illusion rather than something anomalous, something unusual and challenging. This kind of scepticism is a nihilistic negative dogmatism that claims we can know nothing at all. The point of positive dogmatic belief is to transcend the uncertainties and vicissitudes of life, of the space-time, flesh-and-blood world of appearances of which we are conscious, by appeal to something nonevident. The point of negative dogmatic belief, what is now called "scepticism," is that there is no way to transcend life in this way. The point of Pyrrhonism, by contrast to both these, is to leave the question open, to say that some kind of transcendence, or experience of what is nonevident, may or may not be possible. Pyrrhonism, it cannot be overstated, is distinguished from both positive and negative dogmatisms in that it has confidence in the world of immediate experience, and remains open to its scientific study and to its pleasures, though alert as well to its pains, dangers, and mysteries. To suspend rather than affirm or deny beliefs is not nihilism but a return to the one thing we have in common, to our problematic but compelling experiential world, where direct experience speaks without need of belief.

—◦◦◦—

Most scholars have perpetuated this confusion between Pyrrhonian scepticism and dogmatic scepticism by treating them as two branches of one school, but there is little evidence to support such a close association provided we keep in mind the shift in meaning of the word scepticism. Indeed, Pyrrhonism and scepticism are fundamentally opposed. Sextus Empiricus, at the beginning of his *Outlines of Scepticism*, distinguishes Pyrrhonism very clearly from negative as well as positive dogmatism. Sextus uses "sceptic" strictly in its original, root sense of inquirer or investigator, literally "one who looks," and he identifies this kind of scepticism with Pyrrhonism. His first chapter is entitled "the most fundamental difference among philosophies," which difference he describes in the very first words of his book:

> When people are investigating any subject, the likely result is either a discovery, or a denial of discovery and a confession of inapprehensibility, or else a continuation of the investigation. This, no doubt, is why in the case of philosophical investigations, too, some have said that they have discovered the truth, some have asserted that it cannot be apprehended, and others are still investigating. Those who are called Dogmatists in the proper sense of the word think that they have discovered the truth—for example, the schools of Aristotle and Epicurus and the Stoics, and some others. The schools of Clitomachus and Carneades, and other Academics, have asserted that things cannot be apprehended. And the Sceptics are still investigating. Hence the most fundamental kinds of philosophy are reasonably thought to be three: the Dogmatic, the Academic, and the Sceptical.[4]

It is important to be clear here (and throughout this work) that the "Academics" referred to are what we would call sceptics in the modern or nihilistic sense, and that the "sceptics" to which Sextus refers are the Pyrrhonists, or followers of Pyrrho, who are not Academics. Sextus stands at the end of a long line of philosophers—arguably including Hecataeus of Abdera, Timon of Phlius, Nausiphanes of Teos, Aenesidemus of Cnossus, and Agrippa, among others[5]—who took as their progenitor Pyrrho of Elis, who as a young man was one of a group of philosophers who accompanied Alexander the Great on his conquests as far as India. In India, as I argue in chapter 2, Pyrrho's encounter with various sages was the likely occasion of his developing his new philosophy, which he brought back to Greece and taught during the remainder of his long life (he died about the age of ninety around 270 BC). Pyrrho's Indian inspirations, I shall argue, are very nearly identical with the outlook of Madhyamaka Buddhists, who also argued for the suspension of judgment about nonevident things. But since he worked in a wholly Greek idiom, it seems reasonable to speak of a reinvention of Buddhism in ancient Greece, rather than a transmission. I shall say more about Pyrrho in due course, and about the striking parallels with South Asian thought, but this is how Sextus describes the Pyrrhonian philosophy, perhaps five hundred years later:

> The Sceptical [Pyrrhonian] persuasion, then, is also called Investigative, from its activity in investigating and inquiring; Suspensive, from the feeling that comes about in the inquirer after the investigation; Aporetic, either (as some say) from the fact that it puzzles over and investigates everything, or else from its being at a loss whether to assert or deny; and Pyrrhonian, from the fact that Pyrrho appears to us to have attached himself to Scepticism more systematically and conspicuously than anyone before him. . . . Scepticism is an ability to set out oppositions among things which appear and are thought of in any way at all, an ability by which, because of the equipollence in the opposed objects and accounts, we come first to suspension of judgment and afterwards to tranquillity.[6]

By contrast, what "scepticism" has come to mean almost exclusively in modern times, and what it had already come to mean to many in ancient times, is neatly captured in Sextus' account of Academic philosophy. The Academics, he tells us, insist that the truth "cannot be apprehended," and in doing so advance a nonevident, dogmatic belief. Sextus cites the Academics Clitomachus and Carneades, as well as their predecessor, Arcesilaus of Pitane, who in the third century BCE turned the Academy founded by Plato in the direction of what scepticism was to become—namely, negative dogmatism—by making scepticism in this dogmatic sense the official philosophy of the Academy. Arcesilaus, Sextus says, "certainly seems to me to have much in common with what the Pyrrhonists say, . . . Yet someone might say that we say these things in accordance with what is apparent to us, not affirmatively, whereas he says them with reference to the nature of things—so he says that suspension of judgment is a good thing and assent a bad thing [which the Pyrrhonists do not]."[7]

The surviving ancient writings we have from and about Academic sceptics—the so-called New or Middle Academy, to distinguish it from Plato's original, the Old Academy—are scanty. A major source of information about the school is to be found in what Sextus Empiricus says about it. Other sources include the brief biography by Diogenes Laertius of Arcesilaus, and his fragmentary biographies of Carneades, and Clitomachus, as well as Cicero's philosophical dialogues, particularly his *Academica*, and various fragments by Numenius, Plutarch, Lactantius, Augustine, Galen, and others. The gist of the relevant material on Academic scepticism is reduced to a mere fourteen pages of text in Long and Sedley's compendium of Hellenistic philosophy.[8] Of these sources, only Cicero can be considered an adherent of the Academic school. Arcesilaus and Carneades apparently wrote nothing; and nothing of Clitomachus' has survived.

A review of this material makes it plain that the scepticism of the New Academy was far removed from the scepticism of Pyrrhonism. The title of chapter 33 of book I of Sextus' *Outlines* asks directly: "How does Scepticism [in the Pyrrhonian sense] differ from the Academic philosophy?" He proceeds to argue that the differences are profound, and that Academic scepticism is a dogmatic view not to be confused with nondogmatic Pyrrhonism. Sextus makes it clear that Academics hold opinions like other dogmatists, as opposed to Pyrrhonists, who are distinguished by their ability to suspend all opinions:

> The members of the New Academy, if they say that everything is inapprehensible, no doubt differ from the Sceptics [i.e., Pyrrhonists] precisely in saying that everything is inapprehensible. For they make affirmations about this, while the Sceptic [i.e., Pyrrhonist] expects it to be possible for some things actually to be apprehended. And they differ from us clearly in their judgments of good and bad. For the Academics say that things are good and bad not in the way we do, but with the conviction that it is plausible that what they call good rather than its contrary is good (and similarly with bad), whereas we do not call anything good or bad with the thought that what we say is plausible—rather, without holding opinions we follow ordinary life in order not to be inactive. Further, we say that appearances are equal in convincingness or lack of convincingness (as far as the argument goes), while they say that some are plausible and others implausible.[9]

Sextus goes on to make it plain that Pyrrhonists do not accept the Academics' appeal to plausibility as a criterion of belief in things not evident: "Carneades and Clitomachus say that they go along with things and that some things are plausible in the sense of having a strong wish with a strong inclination, where we say so in the sense of simply yielding without adherence, in this respect too we differ from them."[10] Academic sceptics like other dogmatists operate with "conviction" and "strong inclination" about even plausible beliefs. They somehow adhere to those beliefs, unlike Pyrrhonists, who respond to experience while remaining noncommittal about even plausible beliefs about the experiences to which they are responding. The notion that a belief might be plausible rather than certain or impossible does not necessarily lessen any conviction one may have about it. Sextus adds that Pyrrhonists also "differ from the New Academy with regard to what leads to the aim [that is, to *ataraxia*]. For those who profess to belong to the Academy make use of the plausible in their lives, while we follow laws and customs and natural feelings, and so live without holding opinions."[11] Plausible belief, in other words, is as much a belief as any other kind. Pyrrhonists by contrast strive to suspend *all* belief in the nonevident, even plausible belief. This approach makes possible *ataraxia*, in their judgment, while the former does not. The pains Sextus takes in his *Outlines* and also in his longer and less concise work, *Against the Professors*,[12] to include the Academic sceptics among the dogmatic philosophers and to distinguish them fundamentally from the Pyrrhonists, show us how important it is to understanding Pyrrhonism that those who practice it not be confused with those who have come to define what we now call "scepticism."

The eclipse of the original sense of scepticism as seeking or inquiring in favor of doubt as its main meaning seems to have been initiated if not completed by Arcesilaus (318–242 BCE), a younger contemporary of Pyrrho's, of whom we have a short but interesting biography in Diogenes Laertius's *Lives*. Born in the Ionian city of Pitane, where he studied mathematics, he came to Athens as a talented young man, and first studied music and then more mathematics, and then philosophy, first with Theophrastus the Peripetetic, and then at Plato's Old Academy. At some point he became head of the Academy, where he apparently remained until his death. According to Diogenes, at least, Arcesilaus was a colorful and controversial figure. "Very fertile in invention," Diogenes tells us, "he could meet objection acutely or bring the course of discussion back to the point at issue. . . . In persuasion he had no equal, and this all the more drew pupils to the school, although they were in terror of his pungent wit. But they willingly put up with that; for his goodness was extraordinary, and he inspired his pupils with hopes. He showed the greatest generosity in private life, being ever ready to confer benefits, yet modestly anxious to conceal the favour."[13] A telling story Diogenes relates is "when a certain youth from Chios was not well pleased with his lectures and preferred those of . . . Hieronymus, Arcesilaus himself took him and introduced him to that philosopher, with an injunction to behave well."[14] He was lavish in his lifestyle, dined well, and, perhaps more problematically, "lived openly with . . . courtesans . . . and was also fond of boys and very susceptible. Hence he was accused by Ariston . . . who called him a corruptor of youth and a shameless teacher of immorality."[15]

On a more philosophical note, Diogenes informs us: "With him [Arcesilaus] begins the Middle Academy; he was the first to suspend his judgment owing to the contradictions of opposing arguments. He was also the first to argue on both sides of a question, and the first to meddle with the system handed down by Plato and, by means of question and answer, to make it more closely resemble eristic."[16] Diogenes also tells us: "He would seem to have held Plato in admiration, and he possessed a copy of his works. Some represent him as emulous of Pyrrho as well. He was devoted to dialectic and adopted the methods of argument introduced by the Eretrian school."[17] This last echoes Sextus' comment about him in his *Outlines*: "And if one is to be convinced by what is said about him, they say that he appeared superficially to be a Pyrrhonist but in truth was a Dogmatist. Because he used to test his companions by his aporetic skill, to see if they were gifted enough to received Platonic beliefs, he seemed to be aporetic; but to the gifted among his companions he would entrust Plato's views."[18]

The clear judgment of both Sextus and Diogenes that Arcesilaus was a faux-Pyrrhonist suggests how a bridge for transporting and redefining the term "scepticism" from the Pyrrhonists to the Academics might have been constructed. By being the first to suspend judgment "owing" (*dia*) to the contradictions of opposing arguments, as well as the first "to argue both sides of a question," Arcesilaus linked Pyrrho's suspension of judgment with an internalized argumentative technique, making suspension, it seems, a function of that technique. He seems to have combined elements of Socratic and Pyrrhonian discourse. Now we have evidence, also from Diogenes, that Pyrrho himself was no stranger to argumentative technique, nor even to its internalization: "On being discovered once talking to himself, he answered, when asked the reason, that he was training to be good. In debate he was looked down upon by no one, for he could both discourse at length and also sustain a cross-examination."[19] What Arcesilaus seems to have done was go a step further and draw the dogmatic conclusion, repugnant to the Pyrrhonists, that argumentative technique was somehow a determining criterion governing suspension of judgment. For Pyrrhonsists, suspension of judgment followed but was not explained by the establishment of equipollence or balance among opposing arguments. Where Pyrrhonists saw only a succession of discrete events, however interesting or repeated, Arcesilaus instead saw a single set of events, "opposing arguments," as the cause of another event, "suspension of judgment." Since no argument appeared to be immune from counterargument, it was but a short if fatal step for Arcesilaus and the Academy to conclude that all arguments had counterarguments. From this it followed, in turn, that all judgments must be suspended, that is, that "everything is inapprehensible," as Sextus summed up the Academic view.

Arcesilaus and subsequent Academicians, especially Carneades in the next century, embraced Pyrrhonian techniques of counterargument and transformed them into a dogmatic criterion denying all knowledge, resulting in a universalizing nihilism. Perhaps the most famous demonstration of this was Carneades' dazzling performance in public lectures in Rome in 155 BCE, where he argued for and against justice on successive days, stunning audiences and incurring the displeasure of Cato the Elder, who convinced the Senate to throw the philosophers, for a time, out of the city. By putting the Pyrrhonist technique of counterargument at the center of their philosophical practice, the Academics appeared to be carrying on the work of the sceptics, or inquirers. Their ability, like the Pyrrhonists', to confute those who held positive views seemed to confirm this. But by transforming counterargument into a criterion of dogmatic belief about things nonevident, namely, that no knowledge of such things was possible, Academics put the techniques of the Pyrrhonists to the service of non-Pyrrhonian, dogmatic ends. Scepticism came to mean not inquiry but its exact opposite, the impossibility of inquiry, and that has remained its principal meaning of the term ever since. Out of Pyrrhonism, the Academics fashioned a dogmatism unique in its negativity, and easily mistaken for Pyrrhonism. Scepticism became a mirror image of Pyrrhonism, strikingly similar, but no more than a reversed and illusory projection of the real thing.

The Academics' guiding spirit was Socrates, not Pyrrho, and it was Arcesilaus who, with the help of Pyrrhonian techniques, dogmatized the Socratic view. The precedents for Academic scepticism go back even further than Socrates. Cicero tells us that Democritus denied the possibility of finding the truth of things: "he [Democritus] flatly denies that truth exists at all."[20] Perhaps the earliest expression of the germ of Academic scepticism can be found in Xenophanes in the sixth century BCE, who writes: "And as for certain truth, no man has seen it, nor will there ever be a man who knows about the gods and about all the things I mention. . . . Opinion (seemingly) is fixed by fate upon all things."[21]

Cicero sums up the approach of Arcesilaus as follows:

Arcesilaus was in the practice of denying that anything could be known, not even the one thing Socrates had left for himself—the knowledge that he knew nothing: such was the extent of the obscurity in which everything lurked, on his assessment, and there was nothing which could be discerned or understood. For these reasons, he said, no one should maintain or assert anything or give it the acceptance of assent, but he should always curb his rashness and restrain it from every slip; for it would be extraordinary rashness to accept something either false or incognitive, and nothing was more dishonourable than for assent and acceptance to run ahead of cognition and grasp. He used to act consistently with this philosophy, and by arguing against everyone's opinions he drew most people away from their own, so that when reasons of equal weight were found on opposite sides on the same subject, the easier course was to withhold assent from either side.[22]

The goal of *ataraxia* was gradually forgotten by the Academics in favor of argumentative virtuosity and self-assertion. The principal Academics, Arcesilaus and Carneades, were prone to ostentatious displays and intent upon public approval. Both seemed to promote and even relish their roles as philosophical celebrities. Pyrrho's disciple Timon described Arcesilaus as a "flatterer of the mob."[23] Even Cicero speaks of his "chicanery" (*calumnia*).[24] All this stands in stark contrast to the quieter values of solitude and general indifference to experience advocated by the Pyrrhonists as part of the realization of tranquility. Arcesilaus, for whom we have some personal evidence, fits the bill of a charismatic dogmatist, generous but deeply egotistical, running to extremes of indulgence and forbearance, assertive but restless, his certainties exaggerated, it seems, to fend off his doubts.

Pyrrhonists, on the other hand, have nothing to prove, no criterion to defend, and only then, having reached that point, do they find themselves open to tranquility. Liberated from dogmatic views, they have nothing to assert or deny, and are content to live on the sufferance of immediate experience (including likely expectations of immediate experience) as it comes to them. Pyrrho after his return from India lived a half century and more quietly off the beaten path, in his small home city of Elis, where disciples such as Timon had to seek him out. The details of his life, so colorfully presented by Diogenes, need not be rehearsed here. He choose not to abide in Athens or some other great center where he could encounter and debate his philosophical opponents, though he did not hesitate to do so when occasion warranted. He concentrated instead, it seems, on perfecting his own practice of self-discipline. No wonder that we know so little about the Pyrrhonists; they shunned the limelight. Timon, we are told by Diogenes, earned his pupils not by trying to catch them but by fleeing from them, and he "was very fond of gardens and preferred to mind his own affairs."[25] A witty, perceptive, easygoing man, by Diogenes' account, fond of wine and good living, Timon also lived to extreme old age. He did live in Athens and other centers at times, but seemed content to let the example of the life he led speak for itself. "[I]n the time that he could spare from philosophy," Diogenes relates, "he used to write poems. These included epics, tragedies, satyric dramas, thirty comedies and sixty tragedies, besides *silli* (lampoons) and obscene poems."[26] Keeping a low but not necessarily quiet profile seems to have been part of the Pyrrhonian lifestyle, in contrast to the egotistical assertiveness of positive and negative dogmatists, with their need for an audience and followers. Nothing we know of the remaining Pyrrhonian philosophers contradicts this picture; indeed, the selflessness of the Pyrrhonian practice lies in very style of Sextus' sober texts, much as we might wish he displayed more of the humor of a Timon.

After Pyrrho's pupils Timon, Hecataeus, and Nausiphanes, the historical record of Pyrrhonism becomes scanty, while the Academics command the stage, contending with Stoics, Platonists, Peripetetics, and Epicureans to sell their beliefs to a larger public. Many scholars presume a break in the Pyrrhonian tradition until it is revived or reinvented under Aenesidemus in the first century BCE. But at the end of his life of Timon, Diogenes offers an intriguing outline of a possible Pyrrhonist succession, which he quotes from two sources, albeit obscure ones: Hippobotus and Sotion. This outline links Pyrrho and his pupils directly with Aenesidemus and subsequent Pyrrhonists like Sextus Empiricus, and suggests that the Pyrrhonists continued as a living school throughout the period. It's worth quoting the passage at length to appreciate the possibility of this tradition:

> Hippobotus and Sotion . . . say that he [Timon] had as pupils Dioscurides of Cyprus, Nicolochus of Rhodes, Euphranor of Seleucia, and Praylus of the Troad. The latter . . . was a man of such unflinching courage that, although unjustly accused, he patiently suffered a traitor's death, without so much as designing to speak one work to his fellow-citizens. Euphranor had as pupil Eubulus of Alexandria; Eubulus taught Ptolemy [of Cyrene], and he again Sarpedon and Heraclides; Heraclides again taught Aenesidemus of Cnossus, the compiler of eight books of Pyrrhonean discourses; the latter was the instructor of Zeuxippus, his fellow-citizen, . . . he again of Antiochus of Laodicea on the Lycus, who had as pupils Menodotus of Nicomedia, an empiric physician, and Theiodas of Laodicea; Menodotus was the instructor of Herodotus of Tarsus, son of Arieus, and Herodotus taught Sextus Empiricus, who wrote ten books on Scepticism, and other fine works. Sextus taught Saturninus called Cythenas, another empiricist.[27]

What exactly, one wonders, was taught by each philosopher in this series to the next? We shall say more about this later, but it should now be clear that it was not Academic or dogmatic scepticism but some kind of practice of nonbelief, what Sextus called a skill, or ability (*dunamis*). It is likely to have been, as we shall explore in the next chapter, something inspired by Pyrrho's experience in India. Its final but indirect outcome was tranquility (*ataraxia*), following suspension of judgment about nonevident beliefs. Pyrrhonism may be unique in the West, but it is at one with certain South Asian practices (most conspicuously Buddhism) in advocating liberation from attachments. Freedom from nonevident beliefs *about* direct experience is a freedom from attachment to them; with such attachments gone, we find gone also the elation and fear such beliefs introduced. Beliefs, after all, project the believer into a hypothetical future whose emotional resonance can become the dominant experience of the present, giving rise to undue excitement and anxiety. We see this in obsession and other forms of psychic pathology. Absent such beliefs, the emotional resonance dissolves and tranquility is able to supervene, or so the Pyrrhonists claimed. The principal Pyrrhonist technique for dissolving beliefs it seems was counterargument, subsequently developed at length into various systematic modes of argumentation by Aenesidemus and Agrippa. As beliefs are dissolved, the confusion between those beliefs and the direct experiences about which we hold those beliefs also dissolves. As a result, the Pyrrhonist claims to see direct experiences for what they are, that is, as unclouded by belief. The Pyrrhonist lives in a different sensible and mental world from the dogmatist, one whose regularities and correlations can be revealed only when unencumbered by the distortion of beliefs.

———❧———

One of the great ironies of Western philosophy is that Pyrrhonism, for all its efforts to evade the label of dogmatic belief, has come to be seen in modern times as the epitome of dogmatic scepticism in its most extreme form. The *locus classicus* of the modern attitude towards Pyrrhonism is a lengthy passage in David Hume's *An Enquiry Concerning Human Understanding*:

> For here is the chief and most confounding objection to excessive scepticism, that no durable good can ever result from it; while it remains in its full force and vigour. We need only ask such a sceptic, What his meaning is? And what he proposes by all these curious researches? He is immediately at a loss, and knows not what to answer. A COPERNICAN or PTOLEMAIC, who supports each his different system of astronomy, may hope to produce a conviction, which will remain constant and durable, with his audience. A STOIC or EPICUREAN displays principles, which may not only be durable, but which have an effect on conduct and behavior. But a PYRRHONIAN cannot expect, that his philosophy will have any constant influence

on the mind: Or if it had, that its influence would be beneficial to society. On the contrary, he must acknowledge, if he will acknowledge any thing, that all human life must perish, were his principles universally and steadily to prevail. All discourse, all action would immediately cease; and men remain in a total lethargy, till the necessities of nature, unsatisfied, put an end to their miserable existence. It is true; so fatal an event is very little to be dreaded. Nature is always too strong for principle. And though a PYRRHONIAN may throw himself or others into a momentary amazement and confusion by his profound reasonings; the first and most trivial event in life will put to flight all his doubts and scruples, and leave him the same, in every point of action and speculation, with the philosophers of every other sect, or with those who never concerned themselves in any philosophical researches. When he awakes from his dream, he will be the first to join in the laugh against himself, and to confess, that all his objections are mere amusement, and can have no other tendency than to show the whimsical condition of mankind, who must act and reason and believe; though they are not able, by their most diligent enquiry, to satisfy themselves concerning the foundation of these operations, or to remove the objections, which may be raised against them.[28]

This is hardly the picture of the Pyrrhonist we get from Diogenes' lives of Pyrrho or Timon, nor is it what we find in the steady and liberating soberness of the pages of Sextus Empiricus. Unlike Hume's fatally distorting caricature, they all promote a serious and beneficial transformation of life. But for Hume "all human life must perish" were the Pyrrhonist to prevail, and though the latter may advance "profound reasonings," these are no better than a "dream" which reminds us of the "whimsical" circumstance that we "must act and reason and believe," though we are not able to penetrate to the "foundation of these operations." Hume touches here upon a deep fear that often attends the recognition of the power of what he calls Pyrrhonian argument, a horror of the apparent nothingness that seems to follow upon the denial of all belief. This deep but misplaced fear follows not from the ancient Pyrrhonian texts, however, but from their confusion with Academic scepticism. It is the nihilism of the Academics that Hume mislabels Pyrrhonism, which he finds "excessive" in its denial of all knowledge. When Hume asks how these people, in spite of their compelling arguments, can be serious, he has in mind the nihilism of Academic scepticism that he reads into Pyrrhonism. Far from leading to *ataraxia*, for Hume the "Pyrrhonian" arguments lead to a kind of psychic depression. And so it has been for most modern commentators, who have followed Hume in perpetuating the confusion of Academic and Pyrrhonian scepticism; for them the Pyrrhonian life without belief (adoxastos) has seemed as impossible as it has seemed irrefutable.

The confusion between Pyrrhonism and scepticism is as common in continental European as it is in Anglo-American philosophy. The key text in that branch of philosophy is found in a lengthy passage in Nietzsche's notebooks, later published as *The Will to Power*, where he tells us, in his slapdash, aphoristic style,

> I see only one original figure in those that came after [Socrates]: a late arrival but necessarily the last—the nihilist Pyrrho:—his instinct was opposed to all that had come to the top in the meantime: the Socratics, Plato, the artist's optimism of Heraclitus. (Pyrrho goes back, through Protagoras, to Democritus—). Sagacious weariness: Pyrrho. To live a lowly life among the lowly. No pride. To live in the common way; to honor and believe what all believe. On guard against science and spirit, also aginst all that inflates—Simple: indescribably patient, carefree, mind. *Apatheia*, or rather *praotes*. A Buddhist for Greece, grown up amid the tumult of the schools; a latecomer; weary; the protest of weariness against the zeal of the dialecticians; the unbelief of weariness in the importance of all things. He had seen Alexander, he had seen the Indian penitents. To such refined latecomers, everything lowly, everything poor, even everything idiotic is seductive. It has a narcotic effect: it relaxes (Pascal). On the other hand, in the midst of the crowd and confounded with everyone else, they feel a little warmth: these weary people need warmth—
>
> To overcome contradiction; no context; no will to distinction; to deny the Greek instincts. (Pyrrho lived with his sister who was a midwife.) To disguise wisdom so that it no longer distinguishes; to cloak it in poverty and rags; to perform the lowliest offices: to go to market and sell sucking pigs—Sweetness; light; indifference; no virtues that require gestures: to be everyone's equal even in virtue: ultimate self-overcoming, ultimate indifference. Pyrrho, like Epicurus, two forms of Greek decadence: related, in hatred for dialectics and for all theatrical virtues—these two together were in those days called philosophy—; deliberately holding in low esteem that which they loved; choosing common, even dispised names for it; representing a state in which one is neither sick nor well, neither alive nor dead—Epicurus more naïve, idyllic, grateful; Pyrrho more traveled, experienced, nihilistic—His life was a protest against the great doctrine of identity (happiness = virtue = knowledge). One cannot promote the right way of life through science: wisdom does not make "wise"— The right way of life does not want happiness, turns away from happiness.—[29]

Nietzsche has read Diogenes Laertius' life of Pyrrho, and offers up a striking pastiche, mixing insight with error. He intuits some connection with Buddhism, but misreads both Pyrrho and the Buddhists as nihilists. The emphasis on weariness and "ultimate indifference" points to a negative dogmatism in the style of the Academics, not the Pyrrhonists. Nietzsche sees that Pyrrho advanced "a protest against the great doctrine of identity (happiness = virtue = knowledge)," but he misses entirely the notion of suspension of judgment, of the idea that we can question beliefs about things nonevident while otherwise fully accepting our experience. A nihilist might be expected to abandon any notion of happiness, but there is no evidence Pyrrho ever did so. Nor, as we shall see, did Pyrrho and his followers reject science; quite the contrary. Nor did they disparage all wisdom, but only the pseudo-wisdom of beliefs, leaving open other, more subtle possibilities. Pyrrho certainly shunned the "theatrical virtues," but was no stranger to dialectics. As with Hume, Nietzsche's horror of nihilism is the horror of emptiness, of the annihiliation that it seems to embrace necessarily. Nietzsche's antidote to this was the affirmation of the will, the construction of some kind of belief, even a consciously fictional one, in the face of emptiness, the last thing any Pyrrhonist would recommend. Nietzsche and Hume see only weariness in Pyrrhonism, not tranquility, nor its liberation from anxiety. Nietzsche's Pyrrho, like Hume's, is a radical sceptic for whom nothingness has become an enervating belief, a kind of living death. Pyrhonism for these influential modern thinkers is buried in the cemetery of scepticism, closed over with the very finality it in fact never accepted. As a result of this profound misreading, we have been cut off from an important part of our philosophical heritage.

—◊◊◊—

Two representative examples of this continuing confusion between scepticism and Pyrrhonism in more recent literature can be found in the works of M. F. Burnyeat and Martha Nussbaum. Here we see scholars confronting Pyrrhonism in detail, yet failing to disentangle it from scepticism. Let me discuss each in turn to explore further how Pyrrhonism could continue to appear so puzzling to moderns. I will then consider a rare self-identified modern Pyrrhonist philosopher— Arne Naess—who nonetheless also confuses Pyrrhonism with dogmatic scepticism. I begin with Burnyeat, who begins his well-known article, "Can the Sceptic Live his Scepticism?" with the same long passage from Hume cited above, to which he adds this comment: "[I]t seems to me that Hume and the ancient critics were right. When one has seen how radically the sceptic must detach himself from himself, one will agree that the supposed life without belief is not, after all, a possible life for man."[30] How does Burnyeat reach this conclusion? "[A]taraxia is hardly to be attained," he tells us, "if he [the Pyrrhonist] is not in some sense satisfied—so far—that no answers are forthcoming, that contrary claims are indeed equal. And my question is: How can Sextus then deny that this is something he believes? I do not think he can. Both the causes (reasoned arguments) of the state which Sextus calls appearance and its effects (tranquility and the cessation of emotional disturbance) are such as to justify us in calling it a state of belief."[31] The Pyrrhonist, according to Burnyeat, has a belief about something nonevident, namely, that competing judgments about nonevident claims can be equalized, leading to tranquility. This contradicts the Pyrrhonists' own claims to eschew all beliefs. Burnyeat claims in effect that Pyrrhonism is no more than a variant of Academic scepticism, of the belief that no belief can be substantiated. Indeed, Pyrrhonism so interpreted was what Hume described as "excessive scepticism," the strongest, most destructive expression of Academic scepticism.

How could this be? Burnyeat argues that the Pyrrhonist goes wrong by confusing contrary claims about perceptual matters with contrary claims about non-perceptual matters. Here is the closest he comes to explaining his view: "The source of the objection we have been urging," he tells us, "is that the sceptic [i.e., the Pyrrhonist] wants to treat 'It appears to me that $p$ but I do not believe that $p$', where $p$ is some philosophical proposition such as 'Contrary claims have equal strength', on a par with perceptual instances of that form such as 'It appears (looks) to me that the stick in the water is bent but I do not believe it is.'"[32] Now philosophical propositions have no immediate perceptual content, Burnyeat tells us, so they must be confirmed or denied as beliefs. The perceptual experience, on the other hand, necessarily commands assent, even if it poses an anomaly or paradox, like the sight of the oar bent in water. As Burnyeat puts it: "The latter [perceptual case] is acceptable because its first conjunct describes a genuine experience—in Greek terms, a *pathos*, a *phantasia*, which awaits my assent. And it is important here that assent and impression are logically independent. For they are not independent in the philosophical case. In the philosophical case, the impression, when all is said and done, simply *is* my assent to the conclusion of an argument, assent to it as true."[33]

It can be argued *contra* Burnyeat, as a good Pyrrhonist like Sextus no doubt would do, that there is no distinction between these cases.

Whether we are dealing with sensations or thoughts does not matter; each is itself an immediate, uninferred object of consciousness, a "genuine experience," an effect (whether it is for us pleasurable or painful, beautiful or ugly, indifferent or motivating, etc.). The thought that "contrary claims have equal strength" is for Pyrrhonists on a par with the sight that the stick or oar is bent in water but straight in air. In the first case, *contra* Burnyeat, we do have an immediate experience, namely a thought which we think, that is, imagine, and which we can express physically and therefore publicly by saying or writing that "contrary claims have equal strength." We might imagine, say, a jury having this thought while deliberating conflicting evidence in a trial. Now we not only can have such a thought, but we can also have accompanying it various *beliefs about* that thought (say, that it is true or false); these beliefs are applications to that thought of other thoughts or sensations, which may or may not turn out to be applicable. The second, perceptual case is no different; here we also have an immediate experience, a sight, say the oar bent in water, and such a sight too is commonly accompanied by various *beliefs about* that sight (say, the thought that the oar should appear straight). Just as the bent oar can contradict our accompanying belief about what an oar is, so our experience of contrary claims can contradict our thought that "contrary claims have equal strength," that is, when such claims turn out in fact not to have equal strength. What is crucial in both cases is whether or not our experiences and our beliefs about them (they way we apply experiences to one another) are consistent. As Sextus puts it: "Scepticism is an ability to set out oppositions among things which appear and are thought of in any way at all, an ability by which, because of the equipollence in the opposed objects and accounts, we come first to suspension of judgment and afterwards to tranquility."[34]

Burnyeat argues that thoughts *are* beliefs, that is, inferences of some sort, and sensations are not. He tells us that "impression" and "assent" are logically independent in sensation (as they are), but that they are one and the same in thought (which they are not). This conclusion, though widely held, need not be held, and is conspicuously not held by Sextus (and other Pyrrhonists) and need not and should not be read into their work. One can entertain thoughts as simply what they are, after all, without assuming that they must *always* constitute beliefs or inferences to some other state of affairs, that is, to still other thoughts or sensations, even if they sometimes do so. Thoughts become beliefs only when they are presumed to characterize *other* thoughts or sensations in the absence of confirmation that they actually do so. I can think, that is, imagine, a unicorn without believing in unicorns, that is, without being committed to the belief that the unicorn I imagine is necessarily evidence for a physically existing animal. I can surely make inferences or beliefs *about* unicorns (say, whether they exist or not in the physical world), and these may be true or false, but the thought of a unicorn *per se* need not involve any such inference. In this way, thoughts are no different from sensations, which we can experience without necessarily having to infer that they *must* represent or indicate some other state of affairs, that is, other thoughts or sensations. Insofar as we persist in affirming that they do so in the absence of confirming evidence, we postulate nonevident entities of some sort. An inference or belief is a way in which I choose to use or apply some thought or sensation I already have. When I apply it to other things, I turn it into a criterion for those things; I interpret those things in its terms. And I can be right or wrong about this. When I persist in the absence of evidence, I have a belief. The point is that we have another option according to the Pyrrhonists—we can also suspend judgment about our beliefs.

It is important to be clear about what Sextus and the Pyrrhonists mean by perceptual things, namely, sensations and thoughts. For Sextus thoughts are *noomena* and sensations are *phainomena*,[35] and both of these can best be understood as direct experiences about which various beliefs can but need and should not be held. Sextus goes to some pains to make the point that in comparing beliefs we compare them "in any way at all," including beliefs about thoughts alone as well as sensations alone, and also about them taken together. As he puts it: "we say 'in any way at all' because we set up oppositions in a variety of ways—opposing what appears [*phainomena*] to what appears, what is thought of [*noomenon*] to what is thought of, and crosswise, so as to include all the oppositions."[36] If thoughts were beliefs, as Burnyeat presupposes, this passage would make no sense. For all we would need in that case would be to oppose sensations with thoughts, which would be the only way we could oppose things with what we believe about them. But Sextus emphasizes the full variety of oppositions between and among thoughts and sensations; his insistence that we oppose them "in any way at all" makes sense precisely because we can have beliefs *about* thoughts as well as *about* sensations, as well as about them taken together. In denying that we can have beliefs about thoughts as well as about sensations, Burnyeat misses the Pyrrhonist analysis of the crucial role thoughts, or imaginings, play as an important basis of belief, experienced prior to any belief we might form about them.

An example may help. Where there are conflicting claims about something nonevident, as in the ancient stock example of competing claims that the stars are either even and odd in number, we must be able to imagine that either an even or odd number of stars actually exists and could somehow be counted, even if we are not in a position to carry out such a count. Whether we actually try to count the stars we can see at night, or whether we are content instead imagining trying to do so, we find an undeniable immediate content, whether of the stars we actually see (*aistheton*) and try to count, or of the stars we imagine seeing (*noeton*) and trying to count. Dogmatists go beyond what is evident, beyond the immediate objects of seeing or imagining, and gratuitously assert that one horn of a conflict is true and the other false; they insist on using one set of experiences to characterize another. Some conclude that the number of stars is even not odd, and others that the number is odd not even. Burnyeat claims Pyrrhonists do the same when they reject both options; he says that "accepting the conclusion that *p* [say, that opposing views cancel out one another] on the basis of a certain argument is hardly to be distinguished from coming to *believe* that *p* is *true* with that argument as one's reason."[37] His assumption is that the Pyrrhonist conclusion is as much an inference to the nonevident as any similar dogmatic inference. But the Pyrrhonists explicitly say they make no inferences to what is nonevident, and it is worth taking what they say seriously. That the number of stars is "either odd or even" is a valid if ambiguous inference for them with regard to what is evident. But, lacking any kind of accepted method for actually counting the stars, they point out there is no ground for drawing one conclusion over the other, even though that is what the dogmatist insists we do. It is only because we can imagine, that is, have the thought that we can count the stars, that we are able to infer or believe that we can actually do so, and not otherwise.

And so it is with our beliefs generally: they are mostly beliefs about thoughts we have, beliefs about how they apply (or do not apply) to sensations. I can see the oar bent in water and I can see the oar straight in the air, but unless I can imagine, that is, think about these, I cannot develop a belief about *them*. Without thinking about them, I can experience but not compare successive appearances. I can recognize that they are anomalous or unusual only if I can compare them, and for the most part I need to think, that is, to employ mental images, to do that. Even thoughts that do not reflect or correspond to sensations—such as the thought of a unicorn, or of Santa's workshop—need to be compared in thought to other thoughts before I can develop a belief about them. In order to come to believe that unicorns and Santa's workshop exist in the physical world, I have to imagine experiencing them as sensations, that is, I must be able to imagine encountering a unicorn in the woods, or actually visiting Santa's physical workshop at the North Pole, with the last leg of the journey perhaps by dog sled. Of course, I can experience certain physical realizations of such mental images in the physical world, as in spoken words or visual pictures or illustrations or even three-dimensional physical artifacts, as when I visit Snow White's castle in Disneyland or put my child in the lap of a department store Santa Claus, but these are mere reflections of the mental images which are their originals, as far as we can tell, and not the "real thing."

This is why Sextus insists that we compare beliefs about these direct objects of experience "in any way at all." An actual count of the physical stars, if it could be carried out, would be the criterion for resolving the question of whether the number of stars is even or odd. In the meantime, the lack of such a criterion for resolving competing arguments is not for Pyrrhonists an inference to nothingness, to undecidability, as their critics maintain, but simply a recognition of ambiguous or indeterminate potentiality, of possible but so far unconfirmed outcomes, given how things stand now. Judgment is suspended and the question remains open. Burnyeat treats this ambiguous potentiality as an Academic sceptic would, as if it were a belief about things nonevident. But it is no such belief for the Pyrrhonists; it is rather a recognition of factual ambiguity regarding not how certain *phainomena* and *noomena* appear to us, but how can they be interpreted. Dogmatist A goes beyond the phenomenal evidence to conclude the number of stars must be even; dogmatist B goes beyond the same evidence to conclude the number of stars must be odd; dogmatist C goes beyond the same evidence to conclude the number of stars must be indeterminate. The Pyrrhonist rejects *all* these conclusions as nonevidential. He concludes instead that the number of stars appears, for us at the present time, to be indeterminate, rather than odd or even, but he does not further conclude, as the negative dogmatist urges, that they *must* be inherently or objectively indeterminate. He does not go beyond the evidence to embrace a belief, but rather gives a report on the current state of the evidence, and no more. It is the dogmatist, not the Pyrrhonian sceptic, who draws the additional nonevident conclusion that the number of stars is inherently indeterminate, and so unknowable. Although he disagrees with the positive beliefs concluded by dogmatists A and B, he is at one with them in drawing a nonevident dogmatic conclusion, something the Pyrrhonist refuses to do.

Burnyeat, like Hume, misreads Pyrrhonism not only as a form of Academic or dogmatic scepticism, but as the worse form of it, where all nonevident beliefs are destroyed, with what are for him disastrous consequences. A Pyrrhonist would agree with Burnyeat and Hume about dogmatic scepticism, but would say, as we have seen that Sextus explicitly does, that it is not to be confused with Pyrrhonism. Pyrrhonists embrace a life without belief, pointing out that it need not be a life without thought or inference; we can, it appears, have a life of thought and inference with regard to our immediate objects of experience, including the correlations and testable predictions made from simple trial and error hypotheses as well as those of the most esoteric science. Pyrrhonists fully embrace the involuntary immediacy of their experience, leaving out nothing. Such a life, however, is not a life of thought and inference with regard to what is nonevident, but only with regard to the evident. This is what Pyrrhonists mean by a life without belief. "A life without belief," Burnyeat fears, would be intolerable since he presumes one's very identity depends upon belief. Belief for him (and so many others) is somehow essential to what it is to be human, to self-identity. A life without belief, he concludes, is one in which "the sceptic must detach himself from himself," so that a "life without belief is not, after all, a possible life for man." Now someone can "detach himself from himself" only if his identity is presumed to be a function of some nonevident belief or other which can be denied. But since the Pyrrhonist, unlike the dogmatic sceptic with whom he is confused, does not deny such beliefs but only suspends judgment about them, he must suspend judgment about his identity as well. But he is under no obligation to deny it.

—◁◈▷—

Martha Nussbaum devotes a chapter in her work, *The Therapy of Desire: Theory and Practice in Hellenistic Ethics*, to scepticism as advocated by Sextus Empiricus. She, like Burnyeat, is suspicious about the claims of the Pyrrhonists: "there is, despite Sextus' many denials," she writes, "a quasi-dogmatic element within [Pyrrhonian] Skepticism."[38] "Doesn't the Skeptic centrally, and illicitly," she goes on to ask, "trade on a more dogmatic set of attitudes?"[39] She zeros in on the hidden belief she suggests, like Burnyeat, the Pyrrhonist cannot avoid: "The structure of the whole [argument] is incomprehensible except on the supposition that the practitioner believes *ataraxia* is an end worth going for by some sort of deliberate effort, and believes that these procedures have a connection with *ataraxia* that other available procedures do not."[40] And finally, she charges: "He [Sextus, or any Pyrrhonian] can conceal the value-commitments of his own procedure only by concealing the alternatives to *ataraxia* as an end, refusing to allow its rivals (and their associated methods) to appear on the stage."[41]

Unlike Burnyeat, however, Nussbaum goes on to take seriously what the Pyrrhonian sceptic might say in response to these charges. "*Ataraxia* does not need to become a dogmatic commitment," she suggests the Pyrrhonist would say in response, "because it is already a natural animal impulse, closely linked to other natural impulses that are part of the 'observances of life'—for example, to hunger and thirst, which 'set us on the road' to that which will preserve us. Just as the dog moves to take a thorn out of his paw, so we naturally move to get rid of our pains and impediments: not intensely or with any committed attachment, but because that's just the way we go."[42] "I see no reason," she goes on to conclude, "why a human being could not live like this."[43] She correctly notes, without developing the idea, that "Skeptical practice has a great deal in common (and may be influenced by) Eastern therapeutic philosophies which provide us with many empirical examples of a detached mode of existence like the one Sextus recommends."[44] But precisely those practices seem to be the problem. The complete extirpation of belief can be achieved, she says, but only at a steep price: "Even those of us who might accept a life without emotion are likely to be disturbed at the degree to which this life lacks commitment to others and to society."[45] "Even Pyrrho had his limits," she concludes: "In one of his most revealing and remarkable anecdotes, Diogenes tells us that once a man insulted Pyrrho's sister Philista; and he allowed himself to get enraged on her behalf, saying 'that it was not over a helpless [or dear] woman that one should make a demonstration of one's indifference.'"[46]

Acknowledging the plausibility of the Pyrrhonists' suspension of belief, Nussbaum, like Burnyeat and many others, confusing Pyrrhonism with Academic scepticism, baulks at its consequences—at what she sees as a "detached" and "indifferent" mode of life—and comes around herself to echo Hume's reservations that the life of the Pyrrhonist cannot be sustained, cannot be taken seriously in the end not because we have an intellectual refutation by which to dismiss it, which we do not, but because people just aren't made that way. After all, what Nussbaum calls being "naturally human"[47] necessarily seems to include, as much for her as for Burnyeat, Hume, Neitzsche, and many others, just that impulse to belief the Pyrrhonists would question, without which human virtues such as "love" and "commitment" would apparently not be possible in her view. But perhaps Pyrrho's reaction in defense of his sister Philista is precisely what becomes possible only if we are to follow, not dogmas, but our spontaneous natural impulses. When criticized for this action, Pyrrho's response, according to Diogenes, was that "it was not over a weak [or dear] woman that one should display indifference," no doubt because Philista was not a matter of belief but his flesh-and-blood relation, someone he was likely to have loved, and so his reply was a rebuke to his critic. Pyrrho's ancient critic, like Nussbaum, Burnyeat, Hume, Nietzsche, and most of his modern critics, misses the point. They assume that the Pyrrhonist must be detached and indifferent in *all* respects, when in fact Pyrrhonists advocate detachment and indifference *only* with regard to beliefs about nonevident things. Philista was presumably quite an evident thing to Pyrrho, enough so to engender an appropriate emotional response on his part, which is exactly what the Pyrrhonists tell us to expect of their own behavior. Far from suppressing emotion, as Nussbaum states, Pyrrhonism allows it direct and full expression.

To be disappointed in the Pyrrhonists for their indifference and detachment is to confuse them with nihilistic Academic sceptics for whom indifference and detachment about *all* things follow naturally from their acceptance of the conclusion not only that beliefs about nonevident things are false, but that even what is evident is subject to doubt. The natural affects of life are accepted, not denied, by the Pyrrhonists. "By nature's guidance," Sextus tells us, "we are naturally capable of perceiving and thinking. By the necessitation of feelings, hunger conducts us to food and thirst to drink. By the handing down of customs and laws, we accept, from an everyday point of view, that piety is good and impiety bad. By teaching of kinds of expertise we are not inactive in those which we accept."[48] He also speaks of "moderation of feeling in matters forced upon us."[49] Must we assume that Pyrrho's reaction to the insult to Philista was immoderate or somehow inconsistent with the Pyrrhonist attitude to life? Not at all. Indeed, it might have been precisely what was required. Just as Aristotle's mean does not preclude strong but appropriation reactions, neither does the moderation of the Pyrrhonists. The mean is not necessarily the literal middle, but rather the point of balance, which could be far to one or the other extreme. Ignoring or downplaying the insult is what might have been immoderate, and it may be that that cannot be appreciated until some nonevident beliefs about how we should behave are suspended.

———

It is hard to find a modern philosopher or scholar of philosophy who has taken Pyrrhonism seriously enough to consider himself or herself to be actually a Pyrrhonist, that is, someone who seriously attempts to distinguish the evident from the nonevident, and to live according to the former rather than the latter. Almost all commentators on the Pyrrhonist texts not only conspicuously do not advertise themselves as Pyrrhonists, but also make it plain that they wish not to be so considered. Of the modern philosophers aware of ancient Pyrrhonism, one who is not unwilling to label himself a Pyrrhonist is the Norwegian thinker, Arne Naess. But Naess was far better known under other labels, particularly as an ecologist, and his Pyrrhonism was perhaps more willing than thorough. He concludes his 1968 book, *Scepticism*, with this rather understated remark: "The arguments I have offered both in this and the previous chapters are designed to give support to the Pyrrhonian sceptic. The discussion as a whole is an attempt, on the part of a sympathetic metasceptic, to defend the Pyrrhonist against various undeserved objections."[50] One commentator describes Naess's Pyrrhonian scepticism as follows: "anyone who knows Naess knows that he will sometimes adopt fairly extreme positions (or do certain things!) not because he considers that his view has any privileged status vis-à-vis other views but rather in order both to provoke others to think through their own position and to encourage openness to a diversity of views. As Naess would be the first to point out, for him to seriously maintain that whatever position he had adopted was the 'correct' one would, in any case, be incompatible with his Pyrrhonian skepticism."[51]

Naess is unusually clear about the distinction between Pyrrhonian and Academic scepticism, and he is perhaps unique among modern commentators in approaching Pyrrhonism as a viable and liberating philosophy rather than some kind of puzzling dead end of human thought. What the Pyrrhonian sceptic is liberated from, he says, is belief in one or another conceptual framework: "From a close inspection of the way of the [Pyrrhonian] sceptic," Naess writes, "it is clear that he tends to avoid commitment to conceptualizations or conceptual frameworks; he will therefore tend to avoid any intellectualization of trust, confidence, and belief in terms of the truth of propositions within such frameworks . . . his doubt concerning intellectual abstractions is so profound that he ends up without an explicit conceptual framework of his own."[52] For Naess, the Pyrrhonian sceptic "simply suspends judgment in relation to any proposition claiming to say something *true* about how things really are."[53] He goes on to add: "Reality is in darkness, but not *necessarily* in darkness; perhaps it can be brought to light; at least he does not know that it cannot. In fact, the sceptic himself may, in his own opinion at least, be the one to bring it to light; he may discover how things really are—in at least one respect. This, of course, would mean the end of his career as a sceptic."[54]

But even Naess, for all his enthusiasm, retains certain dogmatic presumptions. He presumes, it seems, that "intellectual abstractions" are the means by which the "truth" of things, that is, their "reality," will be revealed if it is ever to be revealed. This appears to be a belief, not sanctioned by any evidence, a dogmatic commitment to a criterion of "truth." Naess, like many others with an interest in Pyrrhonism, continues at some level to maintain the presumption that truth and knowledge are the products of conceptualization, that is, of thinking in the sense of some kind of abstractive or generalizing activity said to be carried out by the mind. No other alternative seems to be open to him, any more than it has been to the mainstream philosophical tradition. Plato and Aristotle, following the Eleatics and Anaxagoras, treated conceptualization as the fundamental human activity without which no kind of order or knowledge would be possible. The Stoics and Epicureans developed a complex theory of conceptualization, and modern Western philosophy seems inconceivable without it. Even existentialism presupposes concepts of "being" in contrast to the flux of "becoming." Through conceptualization, it is presumed, we bring order out of chaos, universality out of particularity, the one out of the many, and so on. We are said to do this by a mental ability, the power of abstraction, which is said to isolate what is common, constant, and unchanging in an otherwise ever-transforming panorama of sensation. The world of immediate experience is presumed to be in flux, fleeting and unstable, and ultimately indeterminate. The mere passage of time in this view destabilizes even seemingly enduring artifacts to the point where we wonder whether their identity can persist from one moment to another without some kind of conceptual underpinning. To the extent that any order can be gleaned from immediate experience, it must be more or less enduring, and of a non-sensible nature, in short, some kind of abstraction, something in which we must believe.

These paradoxes and puzzles of knowledge are familiar enough to scholars of Western philosophy, and indeed to any student taking an introductory philosophy course, and Naess reflects their enduring dogmatic reach:

> if my previous analyses are adequate, the Pyrrhonian questions all knowledge claims, including those which, in a more recent terminology, may be called "knowledge claims that do *not* go beyond immediate experience." Immediate experience in itself, he tells us, must be chaotic, incomprehensible. The Pyrrhonist "acquiesces in the appearances" not because of any truth or adequate cognitive status that he attaches to the . . . messages which convey the appearances but because such messages convey no knowledge claim at all.[55]

Naess's "messages" that convey appearances are sensations, that is, sensory objects of experience: our sights, sounds, touches, tastes, and smells.

But for Naess and most philosophers these objects or appearances are already said to be constructs, abstractions, forms of some sort: a table, a person, a landscape, etc. Given this, no knowledge of the stuff of the "messages" is possible, or as Naess put it, "claims that do *not* go beyond immediate experience," that is, claims of immediate experience itself, are subject to doubt. As we approach the pure sensory realm, order dissolves into chaos, and knowledge into incoherence.

Insofar as Naess and virtually all Western philosophers presume that sensory appearances are some kind of nonevident synthesis of form and content, that is, something other than what they appear to be, and insofar as they further presume that thoughts or forms are inferences or abstractions which alone enable us to bring order out of the chaos of sensory appearances or content, then it is hard to avoid some kind of dogmatism and nearly impossible to make much sense out of Pyrrhonism. Having lost confidence in the reliability or integrity of sensations as in themselves sufficient or at least indispensable guides to life, mainstream philosophers ancient and modern have hoped to find that guide in some extrasensory notion or form or essence or abstract entity of some sort underlying appearances. But, in both ancient and modern times, dogmatic philosophers found themselves blindsided by the arguments unleashed by both Pyrrhonians and dogmatic sceptics. The result, for mainstream philosophy, has been to transform the dream (Descartes' dream preeminently) of a definitive conceptual understanding of experience into an ever-receding mirage. The choices for mainstream philosophers have been either to soldier on, hoping to come up with the "right" conceptualizations, or to give into the despair felt by Hume at the prospect of negative or dogmatic scepticism, that is, that no such knowledge could ever be attained. The nondogmatic Pyrrhonian alternative, however, has been a road not taken, and hardly considered. It is high time to reintroduce and reconsider it.

—⟊⟊⟊—

We will examine in detail in subsequent chapters the principal Pyrrhonist texts, and the way of life they present. The point here is to emphasize not only their insistence upon suspending belief, whether positive or negative, but also their embrace of immediate experience, of sensations and thoughts, including the plausible anticipation of further immediate experience. Dogmatists then and now, as we have seen, have not been content with sensations as such; they have recoiled in fear from their apparent instability, fleetingness and uncertainty, taking refuge in one or another thought advanced as a belief about sensations (that they are Aristotelian substances, or atoms in the void, or objects in Newtonian absolute space and time, or sense data, or neural impulses, etc.). The variety and complexity of the immediate objects of experience, their apparently contrary and contradictory effects, their predictive variability, their apparently arbitrary status, all these have made such objects problematic for dogmatists. They have refused, as it were, to take sensible, and even mental, experience at face value. They maintain that our direct experiences need some kind of independent explanation, and that this can be achieved only by postulating beyond them some independent controlling reality; this reality, they claim, is what makes our direct objects of experience what they are for us. That Pyrrhonists, by contrast, choose to embrace the immediate objects of experience on their own terms, and to question beliefs projected onto those objects, has struck dogmatic philosophers as no less than astonishing, even incomprehensible, as we have seen with Hume, Nietzsche, Burnyeat, Nussbaum, and even the proclaimed Pyrrhonist, Naess. Part of the burden of this work is to render plausible this confidence of the Pyrrhonists in appearances, and the first step to that end is to distinguish Pyrrhonism from scepticism as it has come to be understood.

Consider the dogmatist's alternatives. When one dogmatic belief in nonevident explanation is challenged persuasively by another, the dogmatist may abandon the first belief in favor of the second, or search for still another belief he or she hopes will trump the criticism. After all, one dogmatism can be replaced by another; if one doesn't work, another might. Facing a host of conflicting beliefs, the challenge to the dogmatist becomes to find the right one, while eliminating the wrong ones. But, when a whole series of such beliefs is challenged, a frustrated but resourceful dogmatist might conclude that no belief in what is nonevident can explain the perplexities and anomalies of appearances. This nihilistic conclusion, however, still reflects and perpetuates the dogmatic presupposition that nonevident explanations are necessary to make sense of appearances, only it now despairs that any can be found. Nihilism seems to have been first expressed in the West in ancient Academic scepticism, as we have seen, with the dogmatic assertion of Arcesilaus and his followers that no knowledge of the nonevident realities informing phenomena is possible. Arcesilaus made explicit what was perhaps only implicit in Socrates, that the only knowledge we can have is the knowledge that we don't have knowledge. This is what scepticism has come to mean in modern times, an apparently irrefutable but barren appraisal of the prospects for knowledge.

The Pyrrhonist's response to this impasse is not to try harder to find the belief (or claim, or theory, or fantasy) that will somehow be able to trump all the others and confound the nihilist; nor is it to conclude with the nihilist that no such compelling nonevident realities exist. The Pyrrhonist instead chooses to suspend judgment about whether or not the nonevident things postulated by dogmatic belief exist. He or she neither affirms nor denies them. Insofar as the objects of such beliefs are nonevident, that is, insofar as they do not appear in immediate experience, the question of their status remains moot at best. For their existence can be confirmed only if they actually appear in the only way it seems they can, in immediate experience, as we imagine they might, and thereby cease to be nonevident; and their nonexistence can be confirmed only if they disappear after so appearing. But prior to any appearance, postulated nonevident entities, Pyrrhonists maintain, can remain only in the limbo of suspended judgment. They may or may not exist in some other world, but without access to that world their status remains unresolved. In the language of parliamentary procedure, Pyrrhonists move to table the question of the status of postulated nonevident entities, on the grounds that no determination pro or con is possible under current circumstances. Dogmatists, on the other hand, wish to call the question and determine the issue, even though the evidence we need to do so remains unavailable.

Suspension of judgment about beliefs, it can hardly be overemphasized, should not be confused with their denial. Beliefs are nonevident, but the designators or signs by which dogmatists hope to indicate them are themselves very evident; they are, after all, no more than certain thoughts we imagine along with certain corresponding sensations, most often certain sounds and sights (spoken words, written words, pictures, models, impersonations, dramatizations, narratives, etc.). Beliefs differ from other appearances only insofar as we take them to represent or indicate some state of affairs that we presume (but cannot establish) exists independently of those designators. A picture of a centaur is a visible sensation representing the thought of one, but it is not (so far) a sign of any centaur existing in nature, insofar as none (so far) have been credibly experienced to have so existed. As we have seen, Pyrrhonists unlike dogmatists accept appearances at face value, as more or less reliable and in any case unavoidable guides to experience. Until the astronauts circled round the back side of the moon no one had ever seen it. Though there were many possible ways of imagining what it might have looked like before the moon trips, these imaginings could be no more than so many conflicting hypotheses about its back side. To insist on any one of them would be to advance a belief about the back of the moon. The Pyrrhonist response would be to suspend judgment about what the backside looked like insofar as phenomenal evidence against which to test any such belief is lacking. Once the back side of the moon *was* seen (and photographed, etc.), then and only then was actual evidence available by which to judge the beliefs hitherto offered about it.

As Sextus says in *Against the Logicians*:

> the Sceptics [Pyrrhonists] very neatly compare those who inquire about things nonevident to men shooting at a mark in the dark; for just as it is probable that one of these hits the mark and another misses, but which has hit or missed is unknowable, so, with the truth hidden almost in the depths of darkness, many arguments are shot at it, but which of them is in accord with it, and which at variance, it is impossible to learn, as the object of inquiry is removed from [the sphere of] the manifest.[56]

Sextus makes the Pyrrhonian acceptance of appearances very clear: "the standard of the Sceptical [i.e., Pyrrhonist] persuasion is what is apparent, implicitly meaning by this the appearances; for they depend on passive and unwilled feelings and are not objects of investigation. (Hence no one, presumably, will raise a controversy over whether an existing thing appears this way or that; rather they investigate whether it is such as it appears)."[57] Most commentators have glossed over this affirmation of appearances, perhaps taking it as some kind of common sense view of things. Yet it is a radical departure from mainstream dogmatic thinking in which, then and now, immediate objects of consciousness, especially sensations, are consistently discounted in favor of other postulated, nonevident realities. Belief in some nonevident reality is not confined to the business of conceptualizing or theorizing experience, which has so preoccupied Western philosophy. It can take on quite difference expressions. Belief in the nonevident is the essential ingredient in the many myths, for instance, through which important aspects of experience are interpreted. A myth offers an imaginative projection—such as the story of Prometheus giving fire to humankind—and postulates that it represents some kind of a connection from the world we immediately experience to another realm (the home of the gods in the clouds above Mt. Olympus), by which the human use of fire can be explained. Similarly, a theory—such as Democritus' abstraction of atoms and the void—is also commonly presumed to represent some kind of connection between the world of immediate experience and another realm, this time an abstract one through which the general variety of immediate objects and their changes can be understood. Pyrrhonism, by contrast, is content to map the more or less predictable correlations among immediate objects which actually can be experienced, and to rely on them not as some kind of evidence for another reality, but simply as the grammar of nature insofar as it can be experienced, the network of its patterning, which we are free to explore out of curiosity if not self-preservation. Nothing further, the Pyrrhonists tell us, seems to be needed.

This is an extraordinary claim. Pyrrhonism is not another view *about* the objects of consciousness, pro or con, as is virtually all of the history of Western philosophy, but rather an acceptance *of* such objects *as* they appear, eschewing through suspension of judgment any attempt to interpret them other than in their own terms. Suspension of judgment is a liberation not only because it removes the problematic burden of defending some nonevident dogmatic belief, but also because it allows us to respond to our direct experience of objects without the distortions, excesses, and denials introduced by unsubstantiated beliefs about those objects. Pyrrhonism is no less than a way of life, one without dogmas, rooted instead squarely in the concrete world of sensations and thoughts. The *ataraxia*, which Pyrrhonists claimed to have discovered following suspension of judgment, is what allowed them to face the world not only without anxiety, but also with dignity and propriety. It is a claim worth taking seriously.

## NOTES

1. Sextus Empiricus, *Outlines of Scepticism*, trans. Julia Annas and Jonathan Barnes (Cambridge: Cambridge University Press, 2000), bk. 1, sec. 102, 9.

2. Richard H. Popkin, *The History of Scepticism from Savonarola to Bayle*, revised edition (Oxford: Oxford University Press, 2003), 17ff.

3. "Sceptic" is only one of a series of labels Pyrrhonists applied to themselves. See footnote 6 below.

4. Sextus Empiricus, *Outlines of Scepticism*, bk.I, sec. I, 3. I follow here the translation of Julia Annas and Jonathan Barnes, who have chosen to render Sextus' title as *Outlines of Scepticism*, in contrast to earlier translators such as R. G. Bury, who used the title *Outlines of Pyrrhonism*.

5. Cf. Diogenes Laertius, "Pyrrho," in his *Lives of Eminent Philosophers*, trans. R. D. Hicks, Loeb Classical Library (Cambridge, Mass.: Harvard University Press, 2000), vol. 2, IX, 69, 483, and IX, 106, 517; also, see note 21 below.

6. Sextus Empiricus, *Outlines of Scepticism*, I, 4, 4.

7. Ibid., I, 233, 61–62

8. Cf. A. A. Long and D. N. Sedley, *The Hellenistic Philosophers* (Cambridge: Cambridge University Press, 1987), vol. 1, "The Academics," 438–67.

9. Sextus Empiricis, *Outlines of Scepticism*, I, 226, 59–60.

10. Ibid., I, 230, 61.

11. Ibid., I, 231, 61.

12. Two books by Sextus have come down to us: the relatively brief but interesting *Outlines*, and the much longer but less focused *Against the Professors*. The latter includes eleven books; in the Loeb Library translation by R. G. Bury, books 7 and 8 are translated by Bury under a separate title, *Against the Logicians*, books 9 and 10 under a separate title, *Against the Physicists*, and book 11 under a separate title, *Against the Ethicists*. In *Against the Professors*, the most sustained discussion of Academic Scepticism is found in book 7 (identical to book I of *Against the Logicians*). Cf. Sextus Empiricus, vol. 2, *Against the Logicians*, trans. R. G. Bury, Loeb Classical Library (Cambridge, Mass: Harvard University Press, 1961), lines 150–90, 83–103.

13. Ibid., IV, 37, 415.

14. Ibid., IV, 42, 421.

15. Ibid., IV, 40, 417–19.

16. Diogenes Laertius, *Lives*, IV, 28, 405.

17. Ibid., IV, 33, 409–10.

18. Sextus Empiricus, *Outlines of Scepticism*, I, 234, 62.

19. Diogenes Laertius, *Lives*, IX, 64, 477.

20. Cicero, *Academica*, trans. H. Rackham, Loeb Classical Library (Cambridge, Mass.: Harvard University Press, 1961), (II, 73), 559.

21. Xenophanes, fragment 34, *Ancilla to The Pre-Socratic Philosophers*, trans. Kathleen Freeman (Cambridge, Mass.: Harvard University Press, 1966), 24.

22. Cicero, *Academica* I, 43–46, quoted by Long and Sedley, *Hellenistic Philosophers*, vol. 1, 438.

23. Diogenes Laertius, *Lives*, IV, 42, 419.

24. Cicero, *Academica* II, 14, 485.

25. Diogenes Laertius, *Lives*, IX, 112, 523.

26. Ibid., IX, 110, 521.

27. Ibid., IX, 115–16, 525–27.

28. David Hume, *An Inquiry Concerning Human Understanding* (Indianapolis: Hackett Publishing, second ed., 1993), 110–11.

29. Friedrich Nietzsche, *The Will to Power*, trans. Walter Kaufmann and R. J. Hollingdale (New York: Vintage Books, 1968), sec. 437, 240–42.

30. M. F. Burnyeat, "Can the Sceptic Live his Scepticism?" in *Doubt and Dogmatism: Studies in Hellenistic Epistemology*, ed. Malcolm Schofield, Myles Burnyeat, and Jonathan Barnes (Oxford: Clarendon Press, 1980), 53.

31. Ibid., 52.

32. Ibid., 52.

33. Ibid., 52–53.

34. Sextus Empiricus, *Outlines of Scepticism*, I, 8, 4.

35. Ibid., I, 9, 4; for the Greek, see Sextus Empiricus, *Outlines of Pyrrhonism*, trans. R. G. Bury, Loeb Classical Library (Cambridge, Mass.: Harvard University Press, 1961), 6.

36. Sextus Empiricus, *Outlines of Scepticism*, I, 9, 4.

37. Ibid., 50.

38. Martha C. Nussbaum, *The Therapy of Desire: Theory and Practice in Hellenistic Ethics* (Princeton, N.J.: Princeton University Press, 1994), 285.

39. Ibid., 298.

40. Ibid., 304.

41. Ibid., 305.

42. Ibid., 305.

43. Ibid., 312.

44. Ibid., 312.

45. Ibid., 313–14.

46. Ibid., 315; cf., Diogenes Laertius, *Lives*, IX, 66, 479.

47. Ibid., 312.

48. Sextus Empiricus, *Outlines of Scepticism*, I, xi, 23, 9.

49. Ibid., I, xii, 25, 10.

50. Arne Naess, *Scepticism* (London: Routledge & Kegan Paul, 1968), 156.

51. Warwick Fox, "Arne Naess: A Biographical Sketch," http://trumpeter.athabascau.ca/content/v9.2/fox.html, accessed October 2005.

52. Naess, *Scepticism*, 15.

53. Ibid., 56.

54. Ibid., 56.

55. Ibid., 34.

56. Sextus Empiricus, *Against the Logicians*, trans. R. G. Bury, Loeb Classical Library (Cambridge, Mass.: Harvard University Press, 1961), (II, 325), 409.

57. Ibid., I, xi, 22, 9.

# 2

# Pyrrhonism and Buddhism

Pyrrhonism seems to stand alone among indigenous movements in the West as a nondogmatic soteriological practice. On a global scale, however, it does not stand alone. Nondogmatic soteriological practices can widely be found in South and East Asia among Hindus, Jains, Buddhists, and Taoists, among others. There are striking similarities between some of these practices and Pyrrhonism. Pyrrho, as we have noted, went to India with Alexander the Great in the fourth century BCE, where he apparently met Indian sages who may have influenced him with regard to such practices. I shall argue here that a very plausible case can be made for such influence. I shall compare the principal Pyrrhonian texts with the principal texts of the Eastern school most similar to Pyrrhonism, namely, the Madhyamaka school of Mahāyāna Buddhism. We shall see that, when overlayed on one another, Pyrrhonism and the Madhyamaka display an exceptional congruity, and that they can plausibly be read as two expressions of the same philosophical understanding and practice. Insofar as this is so, each can be used to illuminate the other, a cross-fertilization that will lead us deeper into the issues involved.[1]

—❧—

First, some history. No one doubts that significant contact existed in ancient times between Indians and Greeks. Some kind of trade seems to have been carried on between the eastern Mediterranean basin and India from a very early date, eventually taking advantage of monsoon winds carrying ships from the Red Sea straight across the Arabian Sea to the west coast of India.[2] The Persian empire by the sixth century BCE included both northwest India and the Ionian Greek city states of Asia Minor. Megasthenes, a Greek writer who lived at the court of

King Candragupta in India as ambassador for Seleucus I around 300 BCE, recounted mythic tales of Dionysius and Hercules visiting India.[3] In 517 BCE, the Greek Scylax of Caryanda was sent by Darius I to explore the Indus River valley, and his now-lost book, *Ges Periodos*, is the earliest known first-hand account of India by a Greek.[4] The earliest Greek map to indicate India even approximately—by marking the Indus River—was drawn by Hecataeus of Miletus (c. 560–490 BCE).[5] By the time of Eratosthenes' map of the world, drawn in Alexandria in the third century BCE, India appears in its familiar triangular shape, with the Indus and Ganges rivers and the Himalayan mountains accurately placed. The Indians knew the Greeks (and later, other peoples from the West) as the Yavanas or Yonas (probably a transliteration of "Ionians").[6] The middle-length discourses of the Buddha include a revealing and plausible reference to the Yonas as a people distinguished by having only two classes, slaves and free men, though the authenticity of this text has been disputed.[7]

Strong evidence also exists of personal contact between ancient Greek and Indian thinkers, though the extent and depth of that contact is less clear. One of the best known instances is the intriguing case of Pyrrho of Elis, who traveled to India with a group of philosophers, including his older contemporary Anaxarchus, in the entourage of Alexander the Great. Our source for this contact is Diogenes Laertius' life of Pyrrho in his *Lives of Eminent Philosophers*. Writing in the early third century CE, but using older sources then still extant, including in this instance a certain otherwise unknown Ascanius of Abdera, Diogenes tells us:

> Afterwards he [Pyrrho] joined Anaxarchus, whom he accompanied on his travels everywhere so that he even forgathered with the Indian Gymnosophists and with the Magi. This led him to adopt a most noble philosophy, to quote Ascanius of Abdera, taking the form of agnosticism and suspension of judgment. He denied that anything was honorable or dishonorable, just or unjust. And so, universally, he held that there is nothing really existent, but custom and convention govern human action for no single thing is in itself any more this than that.[8]

Diogenes reminds us that Pyrrho was commonly acknowledged as the founder of the ancient Greek sceptical school which bears his name.[9] Pyrrhonists were skilled in refuting claims about what is non-evident, claims they called dogmatic (from *dokein*, to think, in the sense of "to suppose"). They did not simply deny such claims, as we have seen; they called instead for something quite different: a suspension of judgment about them. Suspension of judgment in turn led, by their testimony, to liberation from the demands of the dogmatic claims and counter-claims in question. The subject, no longer constrained by the imperatives of such claims, is said to gain an astonishing release from suffering, a new kind of independence or tranquility (*ataraxia*). Pyrrhonists distinguished themselves, as we have seen, from the Academic sceptics (including Arcesilaus, Carneades, Philo, and Cicero). Academic sceptics seem to have adopted suspension of judgment with regard to many dogmatic claims, but drew from this, unlike the Pyrrhonists, the negative dogmatic conclusion that no knowledge was possible. While details of these intra-sceptic disputes are mostly lacking, it seems that the Pyrrhonists went further than the Academics in their search for liberation. They seem to have focused more consistently and thoroughly on suspension of judgment as a necessary condition for gaining liberation, even to the point of insisting upon suspending judgment about their own suspension of judgment. The claim by Diogenes Laertius that Pyrrho was led to adopt his "most noble philosophy" after contacts with Indian sages, given the emphasis by certain schools in India on suspending belief as a precondition of liberation (as we shall see below), suggests that a closer investigation into the Indian connection might be illuminating for Pyrrhonian philosophy, and for ancient South Asian thought and practice as well. The Buddha himself, like the Pyrrhonists but unlike the Academic sceptics, took a radically undogmatic stance with regard to metaphysical or speculative beliefs, famously neither affirming nor denying them, but rather suspending judgment about them and concentrating instead on practices aimed at easing suffering.[10]

—⁓⁓⁓—

Pyrrho's role as a potential link between Indian philosophy and Greek scepticism has been duly noted by most scholars, but they have generally downplayed its significance. One recent scholar, Richard Bett, has argued at length in his recent study, *Pyrrho, his Antecedents, and his Legacy*, that Pyrrho was not even a Pyrrhonist. Any connection through Pyrrho with South Asian thought, Bett says, was highly unlikely, mostly due to difficulties of translation, particularly "at a detailed doctrinal level."[11] While translation difficulties should not be minimized, the possibility of adequate translation should not be dismissed out of hand, especially given the long history of contact between the Mediterranean and India; we just do not know enough to draw conclusions on this point.[12] And the Pyrrhonist insight, we should remember, is not a "doctrinal" matter at all, but a distinctive attitude that can be variously if indirectly communicated, perhaps in a single moment of illumination. Bett's more important claim, that Pyrrho was no Pyrrhonist, would preclude any role for him as a transmitter of Indian ideas, which might have been crucial for the later Pyrrhonian tradition. His case rests mainly on a reading of a short fragment from Aristocles of Messana, a second-century CE Peripatetic, quoted by the church father Eusebius in the fourth century. The quotation itself paraphrases a summary of Pyrrho's views attributed to his disciple, Timon. The relevant passage is translated by Bett as follows:

> It is necessary above all to consider our own knowledge; for if it is our nature to know nothing, there is no need to enquire any further into other things. There were some among the ancients, too, who made this statement, whom Aristotle has argued against. Pyrrho of Elis was also a powerful advocate of such a position. He himself had left nothing in writing; his pupil Timon, however, says that the person who is to be happy must look to these three points: first, what are things like by nature? Second, in what way ought we to be disposed towards them? and finally, what will be the result for those who are so disposed? He [Timon] says that he [Pyrrho] reveals that things are equally indifferent and unstable and indeterminate; for this reason neither our sensations nor our opinions tell the truth or lie. For this reason, then, we should not trust them, but should be without opinions and without inclinations and without wavering, saying about each single thing that it no more is than is not or both is and is not or neither is nor is not.[13]

In Aristocles we see an early instance of the confusion between Academic scepticism and Pyrrhonism discussed in the last chapter. Bett, following the commentary on this passage by Long and Sedley,[14] notes that Aristocles attributes to Pyrrho the dogmatic view "that any given sensation, or any given opinion, is neither true nor false; and this is the crux of my argument."[15] Bett concludes that

> he [Pyrrho] holds a metaphysical position—reality is inherently indeterminate; his prescription that we should avoid opinions is based precisely on his adherence to this metaphysical position, which . . . he may be understood to regard as itself *more* than mere opinion. He also tells us to employ a form of words reflecting the utter indefiniteness of things. And again, this is not a matter of our being told to refrain from any attempt to describe how things are—as the *epochē* of later Pyrrhonism would lead us to expect. Rather we are being told that we *should* describe how things are, namely, by using this complicated formula reflecting utter indefiniteness. . . . Pyrrho's recommended form of speech does involve a commitment concerning the real natures of things; it attributes no definite characteristics to

things precisely because it expresses a commitment to the thesis that, in their real natures, things *have* no definite characteristics. [Bett's emphasis][16]

This is not the place to debate Bett's lengthy and, by his own admission, sometimes "tortuous"[17] arguments in favor of his thesis; they are based largely on his interpretation of the fragment from Aristocles, whose meaning and reliability remain subject to dispute. Aristocles, whose lost history of philosophy Eusebius quotes, was a Peripatetic philosopher, what Pyrrhonists would call a dogmatist, one clearly unaccepting of the Pyrrhonian attitude, and more important, not likely to understand it even if trying to be accurate. Pyrrhonian scepticism seems to make little or no sense to dogmatists; they can characterize it, it appears, only as a negative version of belief, as nihilism. And indeed, Aristocles follows Aristotle and identifies sceptics as those who hold that "it is our nature to know nothing," and that "neither our sensations nor our opinions tell the truth or lie." Aristocles misses the key point that the Pyrrhonists did not claim to know nothing. They claimed direct knowledge at least of appearances, of our direct sensations and thoughts, and of reasonable inferences from these to other appearances equally direct, with whom they can be reliably if not absolutely correlated—as smoke can reliably if not absolutely be correlated with fire. This is all quite apart from whether or not any of these appearances might also be understood to "tell the truth or lie" about what does not appear. What Pyrrhonists questioned were not appearances as such, but various judgments and beliefs held *about* appearances. As Diogenes puts it in his life of Pyrrho, speaking as if he were himself a Pyrrhonist: "For we admit that we see, and we recognize that we think this or that, but how we see or how we think we know not."[18] Aristocles in this light seems a poor witness concerning Pyrrho and the Pyrrhonists, one whose own dogmatic mode of thought appears to prevent his understanding of the Pyrrhonists on their own terms. It is hard to see how invoking him can be used to discount the well informed and sympathetic testimony of Diogenes.

The point of Pyrrho's advocating a "form of words reflecting the utter indefiniteness of things" is precisely that such a form of words is not descriptive, cannot be descriptive, since what is indeterminate cannot by definition be described. It is not all of reality which is indeterminate, but only that which is other than what we see, think, hear, etc. Appearances really appear; it is just that we do not seem to have a clue how or why they do so, or why we react to them as we do. For Pyrrhonian sceptics there is no using words to describe some reality of indeterminateness; rather, they use words to liberate themselves and others from trying to describe the indeterminate as if it were determinate, that is, some kind of specific object of knowledge. Asserting that such words must somehow anyway be descriptive and indicative of something, as Bett does, only begs the question, which is whether or not language can have nonassertive, nondescriptive, liberative uses. Like Aristocles, Bett imposes a dogmatic standard, that words must be descriptive of something or make no sense. For Bett, and many others, what appears to be nonfactual, nondescriptive, nonindicative language to be meaningful must somehow be made factual, descriptive, and indicative. Indeterminateness must be something, or nothing.[19]

It seems to have been obvious to the tradition which followed Pyrrho and hailed him as their progenitor that the unusual form of speech apparently recommended by Pyrrho had indeed a peculiar and important use, as we shall see further, but not as an indicative assertion of fact. If Pyrrho's real project was to "describe how things are," as Bett and others claim, simple indicative language would have sufficed; there would have been no need for the "special form of words" Bett tries so hard to explain away, the "complex," paradoxical, nonindicative language attributed to Pyrrho which lies at the very heart of his philosophy. This nonindicative language proceeds through caveat, a performative not an indicative mode. After checkmating their dogmatic opponents by posing contradictory arguments, Pyrrhonists warn all concerned that they, as Diogenes puts it, "themselves laid down nothing definitely, not even the laying down of nothing."[20] There were a series of such well known Pyrrhonian caveats, including some listed by Diogenes: "'Not more (one thing than another),' and 'Every saying has its corresponding opposite.'"[21] The effect of such a caveat, as Diogenes puts it, is "that after destroying others it turns round and destroys itself, like a purge which drives the substance out and then in its turn is itself eliminated and destroyed."[22] This self-cancelling move was to the Pyrrhonists their distinguishing feature, the mark of the mature or fully developed practice of suspension of judgment. The clear consensus of Diogenes and the sources he quotes seems to be that this was present and evident first of all in Pyrrho. The Pyrrhonist's caveats are reminders to all that his or her counterarguments are neutralizing, not definitive, insofar as it remains open to either side to advance further arguments. Rather than claim victory, then, or admit defeat, the Pyrrhonian sceptic suggests the stalemated game be suspended. Such caveats were used by the Pyrrhonists to preserve suspension of judgment, making clear their doubt about pursuing "how" or "why" questions ranging beyond what can be directly experienced.

It is curious that Bett, along with most scholars, advances a philosophical view of Pyrrho that stands in direct contradiction not only to the whole later Pyrrhonian tradition (as he acknowledges), but also (as we shall see) to the South Asian schools which may have decisively influenced Pyrrho, and hold to a remarkably similar practice. It is curious because later Pyrrhonists were nothing if not alive to an extraordinary degree to the nuances of dogmatism and determinate beliefs, and it seems implausible that they, with access to important sources about Pyrrho unavailable to modern scholars, would have retrospectively chosen what, in Bett's view, would have been a rather conventional dogmatic thinker as their progenitor. As Bett puts it: "Pyrrho's philosophy, understood as I have proposed, will turn out to be by no means extraordinary for its time and place."[23] Why then would later Pyrrhonists have bothered with Pyrrho at all? There would have been nothing "Pyrrhonian" about him to justify their interest. What I wish to explore, by contrast, is what I suspect remains the more plausible and fruitful thesis, namely, that Pyrrho was indeed the progenitor of the tradition that carried on in his name, and that a significant and perhaps determinative influence in the creation of that extraordinary tradition came from his contacts with Indian sages, just as Diogenes Laertius reports. This is not to say that Pyrrhonism sprang up fully engaged in all respects with Pyrrho, but it is to suggest that the core of mature Pyrrhonist practice—suspension of judgement about beliefs (including a suspension of judgment about beliefs about suspension of judgment), coupled with the consequent experience of *ataraxia*—seems likely to have originated with Pyrrho in the West, and very plausibly to have been derived by him from his Indian sources.

—◁/◁/◁▷—

Let us turn to the "Indian connection." Perhaps the most important discussion to date of Indian influences on Pyrrho is to be found in Everard Flintoff's seminal 1980 article, "Pyrrho and India."[24] Flintoff makes a strong case for the importance of Indian influences on Pyrrho. As he puts it: "if we view the philosophy of Pyrrho not as a series of atomically separate positions some of which could have been taken from equally detached positions in earlier Greek philosophy, but as a rather idiosyncratic organic whole then there are some remarkable affinities with one or more of the schools which seem to have been in existence in India by the time that Pyrrho paid his visit there and that it is at least possible that Pyrrho derived the general shape of his philosophy from these."[25] In particular, Flintoff notes the similarity between Pyrrho's agnosticism and suspension of judgment and the

Buddha's refusal to countenance beliefs about the nature of things, including his insistence that such beliefs were to be neither affirmed nor denied. In both Buddhism and Pyrrhonian scepticism, Flintoff points out, some kind of liberation from suffering is the goal, and it is achieved by resisting assent to any identification with extreme or dogmatic views or beliefs, whether affirmative or negative, which go beyond what is self-evident.[26] Such views overvalue or undervalue ordinary experience, our *phainomena* and *noomena*, and so either way lead to the anxiety and suffering which follow upon most such mismatches between speculation and experience. As a practical therapy and antidote to such views, both Buddhists and Pyrrhonists advocate steering a middle course through life, taking experiences at face value, and avoiding unsubstantiated beliefs or conclusions, neither affirming nor denying them. There is neither some ultra-reality underlying *phainomena* and *noomena* (sensations and thoughts), they suggest, nor are *phainomena* and *noomena* nothing at all; rather they seem to be a curious sort of semi-determinative, semi-indeterminative kind of experience.

Flintoff emphasizes "the antithetical approach towards all metaphysical, indeed perhaps all assertion,"[27] which he finds to be shared to a unique degree by Pyrrhonists with Buddhist and—to some extent—other South Asian schools. It is what sets Pyrrhonists apart, he says, not so much as a technique of disputation (for other Greek schools too were disputatious), but as a technique used as a means to liberation (rather than victory over an opponent). This, Flintoff says, is "at the very heart of the matter."[28] Greek philosophers before Pyrrho used many dialectical techniques to counter the arguments of their opponents, but not, it seems, for the purpose of suspending beliefs. And while some earlier philosophers, especially Democritus and his followers, emphasized some form of personal tranquillity as a goal, they remained very much dogmatic philosophers with strong views about nonevident reality (atoms and the void, etc.). Democritus' favorite term for this goal was *euthymia* (cheerfulness), and it seems likely that he understood it to result from holding the "correct" dogmatic views, such as his own. Indeed, any dogmatist would expect to derive personal satisfaction or well-being from his or her views, and Democritus seems to have emphasized this. But what no dogmatist could do, according to the Pyrrhonists, is achieve *ataraxia*. This practice, derived from India according to Flintoff, is what distinguishes the Pyrrhonists from their Greek predecessors. Although some scholars have tried to link Democritean *euthymia* with *ataraxia*, there seems to be no clear evidence that Democritus (or any philosopher before Pyrrho) used the term *ataraxia* in anything like the Pyrrhonist sense.[29]

For the Pyrrhonist *ataraxia* is not simply cheerfulness, or good spirits, or self-satisfaction, which indeed can accompany the adoption of various beliefs; it is rather a certain unusual and profound freedom from agitation or anxiety, a special tranquility which follows only from having no beliefs at all. *Euthymia*, insofar as it is rooted in a "correct view," in an attachment, is vulnerable to the refutation of that view, hence its instability, which produces anxiety in the believer. For Pyrrhonists, like Buddhists and other nondogmatic soteriological schools, attachment is a symptom of a problem, not a solution. But *ataraxia*, free of any link to a view or attachment, escapes this burden; it is quite a different response to the claims of beliefs, and Flintoff proposes that it is for this reason that *ataraxia* was introduced by the Pyrrhonists in place of *euthymia* and other similar terms, such as *eudaimonia*. *Ataraxia* is not the elation of finding the hidden "truth" underlying experience, nor the security offered by a belief in such a truth, but is instead a liberation from the urge to seek such "truths" or beliefs at all. Insofar as *ataraxia* follows only upon such a suspension of belief, and not upon the adoption of any belief, it could not have been experienced by dogmatists like Epicureans, Stoics, Aristotelians, Platonists, Academic Sceptics, etc. *Ataraxia* is not achieved by replacing an apparently discredited belief with a supposedly better one, but only by suspending *all* beliefs. This sense of *ataraxia* seems to have been what the Pyrrhonists themselves thought distinguished them from the dogmatists, including Epicureans and Stoics who later adopted the term but continued to presume, as in the case of *euthymia*, that it could be realized in a dogmatic context.

It is central to Pyrrhonist and Buddhist and other South Asian practices, and perhaps to any nondogmatic soteriological practice, as we shall see, to formulate various antinomies of belief in order to make them disappear, or cancel out one another, the aim and consequence of this process being to provide an opportunity for a certain tranquillity to supervene. Suspension of judgment about nonevident things in the context of liberation is already evident in the Buddha's striking refusal to speculate about such matters.[30] "Now the harnessing of doubt to a goal of this sort," Flintoff says, "seems to me to be without precedent in Greek thought."[31] Before Pyrrho, Flintoff says, the point was to confuse one's adversary, clearing the way for the promulgation of a competing view or belief: "In the pre-Socratics, the Sophists and the Dialogues of Plato, *aporia* [disputation] is merely a means to an end. In Pyrrho, on the contrary, it is something like an end in itself—it is the only way by which to attain the new level of tranquil consciousness."[32] The Socrates of the Platonic dialogues, one might object, may have had a sense of *aporia* as an end in itself, as a necessary therapy for dissolving dogmatic views, leading to a kind of tranquility that Socrates personally seems to have displayed. Or this may have been a claim later made about Socrates by Academic sceptics, beginning with Arcesilaus, as Harald Thorsrud suggests in his "Ancient Greek Skepticism."[33] But, as far as I know, this is nowhere explicitly stated about Socrates by later Greek writers; rather it seems at best left as an implication to be drawn from his example. And Socrates famously claimed to know something, namely, that he knew nothing, and so had a kind of conceit, or passion, a dogmatic belief. For the Academic, Socrates' claim that he knew nothing morphs into the claim that nothing can be known. This, as we have suggested, is the mark of the Academic rather than the Pyrrhonian sceptic, with the latter claiming it leads to anxiety rather than tranquillity. Flintoff points out that we have to wait for Pyrrho's use of the term *ataraxia* (freedom from passion, calmness, tranquility) to make this result explicit in Greek thought. He reminds us, moreover, that a complex vocabulary for states variously free of belief (*ahiṃsā, advaita, nirvāṇa, ānanda, samādhi, bodhi, chit, mokṣa, sat*) existed early on in India among virtually all major schools.[34]

Flintoff also points out that, in addition to Buddhism, there existed in India a developed and autonomous sceptical tradition associated with the obscure figure of Sañjaya Belatthiputta, roughly a contemporary of the Buddha, which also might have been able to inform Pyrrho's philosophy. We are told by Diogenes only that Pyrrho spoke with "gymnosophists" (literally, naked philosophers, perhaps *sādhus* or itinerant holy men of some sort), and "magi" (or magicians, or wise men, or sages). The latter might have been anyone, including Sañjayan sceptics or, more likely, early Buddhists. Our meager knowledge of Sañjayan scepticism comes mostly from a few obscure Jain and Buddhist texts written centuries later, particularly Silanka's commentary on the *Sūtrakṛtāṅga*, where, Flintoff points out, sixty-seven different types of Sceptic are distinguished.[35] According to one scholar, Hiralal Jain, "Sañjaya Belatthiputta was the preacher of *Ajñāvāda* or Agnosticism. He says that if 'you asked me, "Is there another world?" and if I believed that there was, I should tell you so. But that is not what I say. I do not say that is so; nor do I say that it is not so.'"[36] It would be harder to express more succinctly the Pyrrhonist attitude than this.

In addition, Flintoff points out that in matters of practice, or everyday life, Pyrrho and his disciples introduced into Greece a phenomenon common in India but previously absent, rare, or marginal in Greece, namely, one of wandering holy men, often possessed of special powers, indifferent to pain and suffering.[37] Pyrrho himself is said by Diogenes Laertius to have gone off wandering, and to have endured "septic salves and surgical and caustic remedies" for a wound without "so much as a frown."[38] We might add Diogenes' story in his life of Anaxarchus, Pyrrho's mentor and traveling companion to India: When later captured and condemned to death by his enemy Nicocreon, the tyrant of Cyprus, whom he had once insulted, Anaxarchus bit off his tongue and spat it at the tyrant, preempting his order that it be cut out prior to his execution.[39] Scholars have traditionally dismissed such tales as apocryphal flights of fancy, but they are a staple of Indian life, ancient and modern. It seems unlikely that Pyrrho and his philosophical companions introduced into Greece a philosophical "lifestyle" entirely without precedent there, given Diogenes the Cynic and other earlier Greek "eccentrics," but their Indian experiences could only have promoted further interest in what we might call "alternative" lifestyles.[40] We see this tradition of eccentric "wise men" continuing in the ancient classical West with popular figures such as Apollonius of Tyana (or even Jesus of Nazareth).

—◦◦◦—

Let me add some observations about Flintoff's thesis. On at least one point of technique, he seems to have overstated his case. He argues that the use of the quadralemma by Greek sceptics, prominent in later writers such as Sextus Empiricus, was "without precedent in Greek philosophical or indeed any other thinking."[41] He suggests it was derived from India, where it was common among Buddhists, Jains, and others, possibly including as well the early Indian sceptic, Sañjaya. The quadralemma expands logical space from simply p or ~p to include as well: both p and ~p, and neither p nor ~p. In objection to Flintoff's claim, R. J. Hankinson points out that "there is no need to suppose that it [the tetralemma (= quadralemma)] is of eastern provenance."[42] He reminds us that Aristotle, writing before Alexander's expedition to the east, refers to the quadralemma in the *Metaphysics* (1028a). Hankinson translates Aristotle's complaint about anyone who uses it as follows: "investigation with this person is pointless, since he says nothing. For he says neither yes or no, but both yes and no, and then he denies these, saying neither yes nor no."[43] Aristotle does not consider, however, that saying "neither yes nor no" may be the point for some.

That the quadralemma can be found in both Greece and India before Pyrrho's time would seem to preclude his role as its agent of transmission. But, as Flintoff reminds us, a number of early Greek philosophers are reported to have traveled widely in the east, including Thales, Solon, Lycurgus, Cleobulus, Pythagoras, Eudoxus, and Democritus (who hailed, like Ascanius, from Abdera, and, according to Philo of Athens, was the philosopher of whom Pyrrho was "most fond."[44]). Most of these figures went to Egypt and Persia (where they might have met Indians at court, in the markets, or at the temples), but Pythagoras and Democritus, at least, are said to have gone all the way to India before Pyrrho.[45] Plutarch tells us of at least one report, by a certain Aristocrates, recording the voyages of Lycurgus "into Spain, Africa, and the Indies, and his conferences there with the Gymnosophists."[46] Herodotus gives us our account of the voyage of Scylax to India,[47] and tells us that "the number of Indians is greater than any other people I know of."[48] These and likely other possibilities for contact and transmission of ideas seem to have existed very early on,[49] as we have noted, and it would seem hardly surprising that Aristotle, who had one of the earliest and largest private libraries,[50] might have been familiar with the quadralemma from some early source he does not acknowledge. The question of its origin is put back, not resolved. This hardly affects Flintoff's larger thesis of East-West contact, however, nor the key role, following Diogenes, he ascribes to Pyrrho. What is perhaps more important about Flintoff's claim is his emphasis on the use to which the quadralemma and other antinomial techniques are put, namely, to bring about liberation, and his suggestion that it is these kinds of techniques with this kind of purpose which are shared by Pyrrhonists on the one hand, and Buddhists and other South Asian traditions on the other. It is in this regard that Pyrrho remains the possible agent of transmission between them.

An interesting item of evidence for Pyrrhonist-type views in India not mentioned by Flintoff is found in the account of Indian philosophers given by Megasthenes as cited by Strabo in his *Geography*. Megasthenes, in speaking about certain Brahmins, is reported as having said:

> that they [the Brahmins, *Brachmanes*] converse more about death than anything else, for they believe that the life here is, as it were, that of a babe still in the womb, and that death, to those who have devoted themselves to philosophy, is birth into the true life, that is, the happy life; and that they therefore discipline themselves most of all to be ready for death; and that they believe that nothing that happens to mankind is good or bad, for otherwise some would not be grieved

and others delighted by the same things, both having dream-like notions, and that the same persons cannot at one time to grieved and then in turn change and be delighted by the same things.[51]

Megasthenes was an Ionian, an older contemporary of Pyrrho's, who was sent on several embassies by the Seleucus I between 302–291 BCE to the court of the Chandragupta, founder of the Maurya Empire in India.[52] He seems to have spent considerable time in India, and wrote a general account of the country, used extensively by Strabo. His remarks, transmitted through Strabo, suggest that recognizing the relativism of good and bad, joy and sorrow, and being freed of them, may have been linked in India by some philosophers, at least, to some kind of suspension of notions or opinions and avoidance of authority. Opinions or notions (*hypolepsis*) are not said to be nothing, nor nonsensical, but are compared to dreams, generally believed to be compelling realities as long as they are being dreamt, if not afterwards. Megasthenes, it seems, can plausibly be read as describing a practice based on suspending claims made for various opinions touted as beliefs. It seems apparent that the aim, as with later Pyrrhonists, is not annihilation of the opponent through refutation of his or her beliefs, which presupposes the continued necessity of belief, but rather some kind of liberation from belief in what turns out to be mere opinion, insofar as it can be shown that opinions seem to entail contradiction (as in the suggested absurdity of believing that the same things can differently affect the same persons). The former approach suggests scepticism as a negative form of dogmatic assertion ("I know that you and I don't know"), while the latter suggests scepticism as a positive therapeutic practice ("we can seek freedom from belief").

In this kind of therapeutic practice, the raw material—the opinions or the dreams, or generally, the *phainomena* and *noomena*—remain; what is dissipated is one or more beliefs about that raw material. Of course, this is not to suggest that the so-called Brahmins Megasthenes describes freed themselves entirely from beliefs, only that they seem to have practiced a method that seemed be used to that end, and that could also have been observed and adopted by a visiting Greek like Pyrrho, who was in India not long before Megasthenes. Argument and counterargument were clearly present, and that would have been sufficient to prompt the radical conclusion (drawn, it seems, by the Buddha, and perhaps by Indian sceptics and others) of suspension of judgment as a means to liberation, rather than as a means for pursuing a search for "truth" about what is nonevident. It may have been that Pyrrho, seeing such a practice, might have recognized how the powerful argumentative arsenal developed by the Greeks could be harnassed to liberation.

One practice on which Flintoff is silent is meditation, also common to all the main Indian traditions, and so central to them that its apparent absence in the West in ancient times should seem surprising if we are to take Indian influences seriously. Pyrrho and his philosophical companions, with all their apparent curiosity, would likely not have failed to notice the unusual and striking activities associated with what we know were then existing varieties of Indian meditative practice. While extensive handbooks of mediative practices were developed in India and elsewhere in South Asia in ancient times (for example, the *Visuddhimagga* and the *Vimuttimagga*),[53] the relative absence in the West of those particular types of practices is notable, until their introduction from the East in modern times. Of course, there existed in the West long before modern times a variety of spiritual practices (prayer, chanting, isolation, mortification, etc.), especially among hermits, monastics, and mystics. But such practices rarely included, it seems, the particular combination of specific postures with specific techniques of concentration characteristic of South Asian meditative practices. Perhaps the closest approximation may be found in the practices of the Greek Orthodox Hesychasts, where "the body was to be held immovable for a long time, the chin pressed against the breast, the breath held, the eyes turned in, and so on."[54] On the other hand, the magicians and sages of the Hellenistic and Roman eras post-Pyrrho may well represent only the visible tip of a hidden iceberg of Eastern meditative practice that did get through, at least in part. We know that Plotinus, for one, practiced some kind of spiritual self-discipline which informed his indifference to suffering, enabled his fortitude, and produced in him ecstatic states perhaps comparable to those of Eastern practitioners. Porphyry, his student, tells us in his "Life" of Plotinus that Plotinus studied in Alexandria under Ammonius, through whom "he became eager to investigate the Persian methods and the system adopted among the Indians."[55]

We should consider, finally, some of the doubts about Indian influences on Pyrrho which have continued in spite of Flintoff's arguments. One recent scholar—Thomas McEvilley—has noted the striking similarities between the Madhyamaka and Pyrrhonism, but questions any direct connection between them. In his work, *The Shape of Ancient Thought: Comparative Studies in Greek and Indian Philosophies*, McEvilley, as part of a comprehensive and detailed cultural comparison, compares a number of passages from Pyrrhonist and Madhyamaka texts, and recognizes their extraordinary congruence.[45] "It is hard," he concludes, "to identify any significant difference between either the methods or the stated purposes of Pyrrhonist and Madhyamaka dialectic. If the pacification of conceptual proliferation (Candrakīrti) and the suppression of belief in real entities or their absence (Nāgārjuna) constitute *nirvāṇa* for an Indian or a Chinese it is hard to say why they should not constitute *nirvāṇa* for a Greek as well."[57] McEvilley's work in this regard complements and supplements the textual comparisons to be offered below. He goes on, however, to discount the Indian influences on Pyrrho and Pyrrhonism: "There is a great temptation to say that Pyrrhon imported into Greece alien and pessimistic teachings from the East. . . . But in fact it seems certain, if one attends to the Greek tradition as a whole, that Pyrrhon must have imbibed the main attitudes of his philosophy from Greek teachers, before the visit to India. The position he came to teach was clearly in the Democritean lineage."[58] McEvilley points out that dialectical argumentation of various sorts was common in Greece as a method for criticizing beliefs, and that some kind of notion of tranquility as a goal of philosophy was developed there as well, especially by Democritus and his followers, including Pyrrho's mentor Anaxarchus. "It is clear, then," he concludes, "that the essentials of Pyrrhonism were already to be found among the followers of Socrates and Democritus in the late fifth and early fourth centuries BCE, well before Alexander's visit to India. If Pyrrhon encountered such doctrines in India, they must simply have reminded him of doctrines that had been common in Greece for a hundred and fifty years and which his own teachers had taught him."[59]

But, as Flintoff emphasizes, it is the harnassing of the techniques of suspension of judgment to the goal of liberation that is the key to Pyrrhonism, and there is no evidence that that occurred in Greece before Pyrrho. It is not at all clear, as noted earlier, that Democritus' *euthymia* (cheerfulness) can be taken to mean tranquility in the sense of Pyrrho's *ataraxia*, not least because of Democritus' own explicit dogmatism. There remains Diogenes' unambiguous testimony, which we have no reason to question, that Pyrrho was led to "adopt" his philosophy because of his contacts in India. McEvilley offers no evidence for downgrading Diogenes' testimony. His unsubstantiated counter-claim is that Diogenes "succumbed" to a "great temptation" by crediting Pyrrho with finding the origins of his philosophy in India.[60] No doubt Pyrrho brought to India a strong sense of dialectical argumentation and a strong sense that philosophy ought to result in some kind of personal transformation—something for which earlier Greek philosophers seem to have been searching, though not necessarily finding. And it seems a reasonable hypothesis that he may have concluded from his experiences with Indian sages, as Flintoff suggested, that argumentation could be used for the purpose of liberation from all beliefs, with tranquility following, and that he brought this novel synthesis of method and goal—already practiced in India by various schools—back to Greece. McEvilley's characterization of Madhyamaka-Pyrrhonist teaching as "pessimistic" and as a "doctrine" suggests a misunderstanding of those teachings. There is nothing pessimistic or doctrinal about liberation from beliefs; as the Buddha taught, liberation is an extraordinarily positive release from suffering. What is pessimistic, in the end, is attachment to dogma, to belief, to doctrine. Before Pyrrho, it seems any kind of liberation in Greece remained predicated on sorting out various wrong dogmas, not in hopes of gaining freedom from dogma as such, but rather in hopes of finding the right dogma or belief in place of all the wrong ones. But insofar as any satisfaction obtained by a belief in what is nonevident remains vulnerable to counterposed doubts, as it seems to be, no such certainty can be any kind of liberation at all in the end, but must rather itself be a form of bondage and a cause of pain. Seeking liberation through one or another belief turns out to be self-defeating. Pyrrho, like the Buddha, taught the opposite: that liberation was possible only through suspending all dogma, all belief.

---

Flintoff's thesis—that the origins of Pyrrhonism likely lay in India—rests, as we have seen, on a number of "points of similarity" between early Indian thought, particularly but not only Buddhism, and what later became Pyrrhonian scepticism. The plausibility of this thesis depends on connecting the dots of otherwise apparently unrelated pieces of evidence. These points of similarity, as Flintoff realized, constitute a kind of evidence of possible direct influence strong enough on its own to be worthy of serious consideration. Insofar as the possible influence of Indian sages on Pyrrho remains an open question, a further comparison of Indian thought, particularly Buddhism, with Pyrrhonism remains relevant. In the remainder of this chapter I wish to expand further the points of similarity between Indian thought and Greek scepticism, adding and connecting some dots in addition to those outlined by Flintoff. I am particularly concerned to draw out points of comparison between the Indian tradition of suspension of judgment for which we have the most evidence, namely, Madhyamaka Buddhism and its roots in the *Sutta Nipāta*, and the most notable Greek tradition of the same, namely Pyrrhonism, with regard to their most important common features.

I proceed by comparing key Pyrrhonist and Buddhist texts. Diogenes' "Life of Pyrrho" and Sextus Empricus' *Outlines of Scepticism* are among the principal sources for the te practice they attribute to Pyrrho's inspiration, and Nāgārjuna's *Mūlamadhyamakārikā* (*The*

*Fundamental Wisdom of the Middle Way*) and Candrakīrti's *Madhya-makāvatāra* (*The Entry into the Middle Way*) are among the principal sources for the Madhyamaka critique inspired by the Buddha. Although these texts were written in the early centuries of the common era, hundreds of years after their acknowledged masters, Pyrrho and the Buddha, respectively, they have become central in many ways to their respective traditions. The practices they describe were almost certainly in existence centuries before, and it is clear that they incorporate much earlier material.[61] Comparing these will bring out important points of agreement in five key areas vis-à-vis Pyrrhonian scepticism and Buddhist Madhyamaka. The five key areas are: method, belief, suspension of judgment, tranquillity, and appearances. I will take up each of these areas in turn.

Let us begin then with method, and with Sextus Empiricus, a second-century CE Greek physician and Pyrrhonist, and author of the principal and by far most extensive Pyrrhonist texts that have come down to us; "what we investigate," he says, "is not what is apparent but what is said about what is apparent."[62] What is called into question here is not language as such, but its use to try to speak about or somehow explain what is otherwise merely apparent. This use of language is questioned by bringing out the oppositions or contradictions it seems to produce. A passage quoted earlier is worth restating: "Scepticism is an ability," Sextus says, "to set out oppositions among things which appear and are thought of in any way at all, an ability by which because of the equipollence [*isotheneia*] in the opposed objects and accounts, we come first to suspension of judgment and afterwards to tranquillity."[63] Pyrrhonian scepticism, it cannot be overemphasized, is not a philosophy in any conventional sense; it is not a dogma, belief, or creed, nor an attempt in any sense to establish or disestablish some kind of conceptual foundation for truth or knowledge; it is rather an "ability" (*dunamis*) to do something, a certain capacity to respond to events positively and therapeutically, a way to live. This therapeutic ability, Sextus tells us, depends upon opposing things which appear (*phainomena*) and are thought of (*noomenon*), that is, which are objects (*pragmata*) and accounts (*logoi*) of those objects, resulting in suspension of judgment (*epochē*) and tranquility (*ataraxia*). Its purpose is to relieve or cure subjects of the suffering caused by the consequences of their beliefs in nonapparent things. And, Sextus makes plain, this is done through the peculiar techniques of questioning and suspension of judgment, after which follows tranquility. These profound and liberating consequences are said to dramatically transform the subject fortunate enough to realize them.

If we look at a classic text of Madhyamaka Buddhism, such as the *The Entry into the Middle Way* by the seventh-century CE Buddhist monk Candrakīrti—who claimed no more than to explain his master Nāgārjuna, the second-century CE founder of the Madhyamaka, "like the dew which coaxes into bloom the buds of an evening lotus"[64]—we find language on method that Sextus could have written: "An opponent is refuted by perceiving that each and every response he offers is nothing but an unsubstantiated thesis."[65] A response deserving refutation, according to Candrakīrti, is any one which goes beyond the self-evidence of immediate sensations and thoughts: "Understanding based on apprehension by any of the six unimpaired faculties [the five senses plus thoughts] is true by the standard of everyday experience, while any remaining reified concepts are false according to this same criterion."[66] Both Pyrrhonism and the Madhyamaka, it seems, accept the immediate and involuntary evidence of the senses and thoughts, and nothing else, at face value. They both resist going beyond immediate sensations and thoughts—or such that might be conditionally but plausibly inferred from them[67]—to make any claims about the hidden nature of appearances, or of abstract or reified appearances, or of matters in any other way construed to be beyond or behind, above or below, appearances.

Let me clarify some key terms. I use the term "appearances" to include thoughts (*noomena*) as well as sensations (*phainomena*), mental as well as physical appearances, as do Pyrrhonism and the Madhyamaka; each tradition, as we shall see, considers both to be self-evident insofar as they actually appear, that is, are present, not absent. The senses include the traditional five modes of sights, sounds, touches, tastes, and smells, while thoughts include what are commonly understood as the "mental objects" of imagination and memory, such as the thought of a unicorn or the recollection of one's mother. For the Madhyamaka any sensation or thought presents as an object (*viṣaya*). There is a certain ambiguity in Greek usage, where the word *phainomena* (to appear, to shine forth) is often used to indicate not only visual sensation, or sensation in general, but also to indicate thoughts in addition to sensations, where both are understood as appearances; it is this broader meaning, common to both schools, that is important to keep in mind. Both schools also agree that while sensations and thoughts are appearances, they can all too easily and mistakenly be taken as evidence of various hyper-realities. These hyper-realities (including their negations) are expressed as beliefs about mere appearances—as when we identify certain sensations as having magical or occult powers, or certain thoughts as representing pure concepts, categories, forms, or other abstracted or reified entities. In such cases, the beliefs in question are taken to refer to something other than or beyond what is apparently real.[68]

The point, as Diogenes Laertius puts it, is that "the apparent is the sceptics' criterion."[69] It is what is "primitive" or "given" in our experience. And just as the liberation of tranquility or *ataraxia* is central for the Pyrrhonists, so does Candrakīrti proclaim a liberation into wisdom, which we know to be ultimately equivalent to the full awakening (*bodhi*) of a buddha, the "tranquility" recognized under a variety of names in the the Indian traditions (*samādhi, nirvāṇa, mokṣa*). "Our arguments," he says, "are just like [a reflection] through which one becomes aware of the possibility of cleansing [spiritual ignorance from] the face of wisdom."[70] In method, we find that Pyrrhonists and the Madhyamaka both proceed to "set out oppositions" between the claims of their opponents about sensations and thoughts on the one hand, and the direct evidence of those sensations and thoughts on the other. They investigate or test these claims, and find them again and again to be unsubstantiated, or contradictory, or absurd, and insofar as they do so they set them aside, suspending judgment, with the surprising and satisfying result of a peaceful liberation. What C. W. Huntington, Jr., says about Candrakīrti and the Prāsaṅgika school of the Madhyamaka applies equally to the Pyrrhonists:

> According to the Prāsaṅgika [school of Candrakīrti] one must be led toward a gradual realization of emptiness solely by means of a critique directed against his own prejudices and presuppositions about so-called empirical experience and the arguments either consciously or unconsciously posited to support these preconceived ideas. The Prāsaṅgika technique is accordingly a species of reductio ad absurdum whereby one moves step by step to become aware of the unforeseen consequences . . . , or better yet, the inherent contradictions . . . that give meaning and structure to every dimension of conventional affairs.[71]

This method or technique is intended to break the bonds of belief, with belief by definition coming into play precisely where direct evidence ends. As the above passages from both traditions indicate, it is a verbal method, one of dialectical confrontation. The interlocutor, driven into contradiction and absurdity, finds his or her belief broken, as it were, and is consequently liberated from attachment to it. A "self," insofar as it can be understood to be created by identification with some belief, is dissolved through breaking the focus and structure of that belief. As the belief is broken down, the "self" it formerly sustained disappears. There are, of course, differences in emphasis and method between Pyrrhonism and the Madhyamaka. The focus in the later Pyrrhonist texts, especially in Sextus Empiricus, is on formulaic canons of argument, especially the various modes (the Ten Modes, the Five Modes, etc.), originally developed by the first-century BCE Pyrrhonist Aenesidemus. These are designed as a series of "talking points," so to speak, to have at hand in disputations with dogmatists of various sorts. As far as I am aware, these do not appear in India in any systematized form, yet many of the individual arguments are similar, and at least one concrete example, the illusion of a coiled rope mistaken for a snake, is invoked both in Sextus and in the work of Samkara, the *advaita* Vedāntist; a more common example, smoke and fire is also invoked with regard to causation by both Sextus and Nāgārjuna.[72] The modes postdate Pyrrho, at any event, and hardly seem incompatible with Eastern verbal practices.

On the other hand, it would appear that South Asian meditative practices, apparently absent in the European West, are primarily nonverbal and solitary. To some, this might suggest a deeper difference. Meditation in South Asian countries achieved a kind of ritualized systematic specificity (detailed techniques of breathing and visualization, postures of sitting, etc.), compelling evidence for which—as a sustained tradition—has not been found in the Greek and Latin West, as noted above. One sits silently in meditation, attending to the contents of one's consciousness, neither embracing nor denying them, and so loosening the bonds of belief. But no fundamental incompatibility is apparent, nor need be posited, between verbal and meditative techniques. In nonverbal meditation, as in Pyrrhonian verbal disputation, one suspends commitment to beliefs about sensations and thoughts; in silently attending to one's internal dialogue, one watches one's beliefs cancel out one another, as it were. As a result, one is led to contemplate not only the absence of these beliefs but the absence of the support they otherwise provide for a traditional "self." Whether some form of South Asian meditative practice played a role among ancient Pyrrhonists, we cannot say. There is no evidence for it, and its absence, especially from Sextus Empiricus, suggests it played little or no part in Pyrrhonian practice. The numerous points of contact between aspects of Greek and Indian culture and thought, however, imply at least its possible existence in the ancient West. Its centrality to the Madhyamaka, by contrast, is beyond question, as attested by both Candrakīrti and Nāgārjuna. Candrakīrti writes: "The meditator sees the emptiness of 'I' and 'mine,' and he will be liberated."[73] And Nāgārjuna flatly states: "Abandonment occurs through meditation."[74] No such statements are found in the Pyrrhonian texts. If I am correct, Pyrrhonism and the Madhyamaka are agreed on key points of verbal methods (putting any belief to the argumentative test, likely leading to a suspension of belief—not rejection—followed by some kind of awakening, enlightenment, or tranquility). And even if nonverbal methods such as mediation did not figure significantly, if at all, in Pyrrhonian practice, they do not seem incompatible with it.

Pyrrhonism and the Madhyamaka, I argue, also share the same attitude toward beliefs. The problem with beliefs is evident in Sextus: "if you hold beliefs, then you posit as real the things you are said to hold beliefs about."[75] Sextus also tells us, quite emphatically, "For anyone who holds beliefs on even one subject, or in general prefers one appearance to another in point of convincingness or lack of convincingness, or makes assertions about any unclear matter, thereby has the distinctive character of a Dogmatist."[76] To hold a belief, according to the Pyrrhonists, is to assert, dogmatically and likely (but not necessarily) wrongly, that some kind of reality lies beyond appearances, existing independently and unconditionally, and that this ultimate reality, among other things, explains what merely appears. Candrakīrti also resists beliefs in this sense: "The Buddhas did not teach that any entity whatsoever [ultimately] exists."[77] And Nāgārjuna, writing roughly at the time of Sextus and Diogenes, tells us: "No Dharma was taught by the Buddha, at any time, in any place, to any person."[78] Nāgārjuna's point may be surprising, given common Buddhist talk of following "the Dharma" in the sense of the Buddha's teaching (the Four Noble Truths, the Eightfold Path, etc.). But the Madhyamaka, like Pyrrhonism, is distinguished precisely by its radical scepticism, by its refusal to countenance any sort of statement of belief, positive or negative, even to the point of calling into question the fundamental tenets of traditional Buddhism itself. What the Pyrrhonists call "dogmatism" ("dogma," from dokeo, that which seems true), Buddhists, it would appear, call "attachment," or "clinging" (upādāna) to a fixed "view" (dṛṣṭi); this means the positing of hidden, unclear, but unconditional and determining entities, so-called true realities that are said to govern our experience.

Beyond their fundamental agreement on method, and on the objects of their method, namely beliefs, Pyrrhonism and the Madhyamaka are also uncannily similar with regard to a third key point: suspension of judgment. What Pyrrhonism calls "suspension of judgment" (epochē) seems consistent with what the Madhyamaka understand as recognition of "emptiness" (śūnyatā), leading to "the silence of the sages."[79] The latter can perhaps be correlated with Pyrrhonian aphasia, or nonassertion. Nonassertion, Sextus tells us, "covers both affirmation and negation," adding that it is "the feeling that we have because of which we say that we neither posit or reject anything."[80] Judgments are assertions about what is nonevident, and suspending them leaves us only with what is evident, now "empty" of any imputed judgmental content. Central to both traditions is their insistence that the dissolution of belief be not a simple denial, in which A turns into non-A, but a suspension of judgment, in which both A and non-A are equally suspended, leaving the subject in a noncommittal state.[81] It is just as possible, after all, to be dogmatic about something not being real as it is about its being real, an attitude characteristic of Academic scepticism. Furthermore, suspension of judgment leads to something quite different, something nondogmatic. As Candrakīrti puts it: "The absence of intrinsic being of [all] things is referred to by wise men as 'emptiness,' and this emptiness also is considered to be empty of any essence of emptiness."[82] Nāgārjuna makes it clear that "emptiness" or suspension of judgment is not just another view of things: "emptiness is the relinquishing of all views. For whomever emptiness is a view, that one will accomplish nothing."[83] And: "'Empty' should not be asserted. 'Nonempty' should not be asserted. Neither both nor neither should be asserted. They are only used nominally."[84] And: "To say 'it is' is to grasp for permanence. To say 'it is not' is to adopt the view of nihilism. Therefore a wise person does not say 'exists' or 'does not exist.'"[85] And finally: "Everything is real and is not real, both real and not real, neither real nor not real. This is the Lord Buddha's teaching."[86]

Compare these passages from Nāgārjuna with the following sequence from Sextus: "nonassertion is refraining from assertion in the general sense (which we say covers both affirmation and negation), so that nonassertion is the feeling we have because of which we say that we neither posit nor reject anything."[87] And: "we shall be able to say what the existing objects are like as observed by us, but as to what they are like in their nature we shall suspend judgment."[88] And further: "In the case of all the sceptical phrases, you should understand that we do not affirm definitely that they are true."[89] Perhaps the most pithy expression of the point is made by Diogenes: "Thus in saying 'we determine nothing,' we are not determining even that."[90] The convergence of attitudes here is remarkable. In suspension of judgment, dogmatists, that is, believers in what is nonevident, are not so much checkmated as stalemated. They can consistently be shown to be wrong, case by case, but that they might be right in some future case is not thereby ruled out. The Pyrrhonists and the Madhyamaka claim not to establish "truth," but only to clean away error, and this only in the interest of fostering tranquillity or "inner peace," a state free of attachment or aversion. In contrast to the dogmatists, they settle for suspension of judgment, or emptiness. They claim no final victory over dogmatism, not least because of the very dogmatism of such a claim. This is reflected in a distinction in Buddhist logic between implicative and nonimplicative negation; in the former, the negation of A implies non-A; in the latter, adopted by the Madhyamaka, the negation of A does not imply non-A.

The fruit of stalemate is tranquility, not another form of aggression. And with tranquility, we come to the fourth important point of agreement between Pyrrhonism and the Madhyamaka. For the Pyrrhonists, as for the Buddhists, tranquility seems originally to have been an unexpected discovery. Having opted for suspension of judgment rather than victory, it came as a surprise to find tranquility following behind, "like its shadow,"[91] as both Diogenes and Sextus tell us. Perhaps the Buddha, sitting under the *bodhi* tree, made this discovery after his final night of anxiety before his awakening, and perhaps Pyrrho, at some point, had a similar experience. Here is what the Greeks have to say about tranquillity, beginning with Sextus: "those who make no determination about what is good and bad by nature neither avoid nor pursue anything with intensity; and hence they are tranquil."[92] Then Diogenes: "No single thing is in itself any more this than that."[93] Tranquility is the discovery, it seems, of the apparent indeterminacy of all things, and the precondition of a different kind of nondogmatic morality. Compare Candrakīrti: "The absence of anxiety [i.e., tranquility] is the distinguishing characteristic of morality."[94] It is belief—some determination of the nature or value of things—which generates doubt and vulnerability, and therefore anxiety, for belief is inherently unstable; it can be challenged, and lost. This does not preclude reasonable expectations about appearances, such as the expectation that the sun will rise tomorrow, but these are not dogmatic beliefs, subject as they are to the test of what is evident or not. And indeed, the sun might not rise tomorrow.

To insist, then, upon some belief is to insist on some unstable and possibly false evaluation, leaving one vulnerable to anxiety and immorality, that is, to self-centered and even self-righteous behavior. And to eschew beliefs is to eschew actions based on beliefs. As Nāgārjuna puts it: "The root of cyclic existence is action. Therefore the wise one does not act."[95] Cyclic existence—the round of ordinary life—is determined in no small part by belief-generated action arising out of self-centered motives (so-called karmic action), so to suspend belief is to suspend such actions as would be generated by belief. What is left, it seems, is the independent, ongoing action and reaction of our appearances. The subject, strictly speaking, ceases to be an agent and becomes a witness, even to the workings of his or her own body and mind. In a somewhat cryptic formulation, Nāgārjuna writes: "There is not the slightest difference between cyclic existence and *nirvāṇa*."[96] Insofar as *nirvāṇa* can be understood to overlap with what the Greeks called "tranquility," it is not another view, nor another place, but rather a state in which cyclic existence is recognized for what it is, the play of appearances, what the Pyrrhonists understood as the ordinary experience of appearances undistorted by beliefs. In this play of appearances, action arises spontaneously as circumstances (not beliefs) dictate; only such spontaneous actions can be considered moral, that is, free of self-centered motives.

Our review of method, beliefs, suspension of judgment, and tranquility, brings us finally to appearances, our last major point of comparison. We have already noted strong similarities here between Pyrrhonism and the Madhyamaka, principally that appearances are at once self-evident and "empty," or without underlying "substance" or "nature," and that there seem to be six senses or modes of appearance. Absent any beliefs, which inflate or deflate and correspondingly distort the value of appearances, both traditions recognize that we respond to appearances spontaneously and at face value. "For we admit that we see," Diogenes tells us, "and we recognize that we think this or that, but how we see or how we think we know not."[97] Sensations and thoughts here are both considered appearances. He adds: "We see that a man moves, and that he perishes; how it happens we do not know. We merely object to accepting the unknown substance behind phenomena."[98] The point seems to be that more than appearances is neither given nor required. Without the struggle to affirm or deny any "unknown substance behind phenomena," those same phenomena are revealed for what they are, no more and no less: "there is nothing really existent," to quote Diogenes again, "but custom and convention govern human action; for no single thing is in itself any more this than that."[99] "Thus, attending to what is apparent," Sextus tells us, "we live in accordance with everyday observances, without holding opinions—for we are not able to be utterly inactive. These everyday observances seem to be fourfold, and to consist in guidance by nature, necessitation by feelings, handing down of laws and customs, and teaching of kind of expertise."[100] These everyday appearances are simply the "empty" facts (*pragmata*) of life, to which we respond as they compel us, positively, negatively, or neutrally, no more and no less. Sextus' phrase "for we are not able to be utterly inactive" has been taken by most commentators as betraying a kind of Pyrrhonist longing for inaction, for a kind of torpor. Yet we can understand this comment as ruling out only actions based on beliefs, while accepting those which arise naturally out of direct experience. Pyrrho's own life, as recounted by Diogenes at least, was certainly energetic enough, as was the Buddha's long life of teaching after his enlightenment.

Pyrrhonism and the Madhyamaka further seem to agree that appearances are mutually dependent on one another. What Pyrrhonism calls "relativism" may be central to what the Madhyamaka and other Buddhists call "dependent origination." Sextus puts it as follows: "since everything is relative, we shall suspend judgment as to what things are independently and in their nature."[101] Things relative to one another, or mutually dependent, are not in any way independent; they have no independently existing essence or ultimate, no individual character or nature. "Whatever is dependently co-arisen," Nāgārjuna says, "that is explained to be emptiness. That, being a dependent designation, is itself the middle way."[102] Dependency seems to be the middle path between absolute being and absolute nothingness. Candrakīrti cites a classic example of dependent origination: "One does not consider a carriage to be different from its own parts, nor to be identical, nor to be in possession of them, nor is it 'in' the parts, nor are they 'in' it, nor is it the mere composite [of its parts]; nor is it the shape."[103] A carriage, or any other phenomenal object, or appearance, is for both Pyrrhonism and the Madhyamaka a kind of "virtual" or "empty" object, no more or less than a bundle of perceptions, constituted both by its various parts, which make it a whole, and by the various wholes in which it finds itself a part. Indeed, every whole is a part of some larger whole, and every part is a whole with parts of its own. What a phenomenal object is for anyone is no more or less than what that person's experience may be of some of its parts and some of the wholes of which it is a part. I see that a carriage has various parts (wheels, axles, a frame, etc.) and also that it is found in various wholes, or contexts (moving on the road, sitting in the garage or repair shop, stalled in traffic, etc.). I can also examine pictures and diagrams of carriages, etc. I need to know only a few of these intersecting phenomenal parts and phenomenal wholes to have a working sense of a phenomenal carriage, the only kind of sense it seems I can ever have. And although I can learn more about carriages, or anything else, and even become recognized as an expert, there remains nothing more, no essence, no Platonic Form, no defining concept, no theory of a carriage or anything else, beyond the level of appearances. To posit any such thing is to invite belief, attachment, aversion, anxiety, immorality.

Appearances, it seems, are no more or less than the steadily unfolding stream of phenomenal parts and wholes, all variously identical, similar, and different to one another.[104] And to realize this, for both schools, is to suspend judgment about speculative or "why" and "how" questions, leaving room only for factual or "which" or "that" questions about phenomena, from which liberation flows. To sum up, for Pyrrhonism and the Madhyamaka alike, dialectical interrogation (the Modes, the Tetralemma, and other techniques, including meditation), leads to a suspension of judgment about nonevident beliefs (claims, cults, magic, dogmas, miracles, theories, attachments, reifications, essences, forms, absolutes, etc.), resulting in a recognition of the "dependent origination," or "emptiness" or "relativity" of the evident (the phenomena, that is, thoughts and sensations as we actually experience them, or reasonably expect to), leading to peace, tranquility, nirvāṇa, liberation, awakening.

—◦∾◦—

Before concluding our comparison, we must consider briefly another set of Buddhist texts, from the Aṭṭhakavagga, the fourth sutta of the Sutta-Nipāta. These texts, the principal source of the Madhyamaka, are considered among the oldest if not the oldest of extant Buddhist texts in the Pāli Canon. Here we find important material concerning suspension of judgment about beliefs or speculations or views, as a precondition of liberation.[105] Consider these passages: "Some people speak . . . with the conviction that they are right. But the sage does not enter into any controversy that has arisen."[106] And: "The sage has abandoned the notion of self or ego and is free from clinging. He does not depend even on knowledge; he does not take sides in the midst of controversy; he has no dogmatic views."[107] The Buddha, we are told, points out that we find things to be pleasant or unpleasant because of the "action of contact, of mental impression."[108] When asked where this contact comes from, he replies: "Contact exists because the compound of mind and matter exists. The habit of grasping is based on wanting things. If there were no wanting, there would be no possessiveness. Similarly, without the element of form, of matter, there would be no contact."[109] The implication seems to be that the belief in form, or matter, that is, the abstraction of concepts thereof, is one if not the key fallacy leading to contact and attachment. What seems clear, in any case, is that suspension of views or beliefs is not only strongly recommended in the most basic Buddhist texts, but is somehow a necessary condition of liberation. Now these scattered but persistent passages in which the sage is said to have "no dogmatic views" stand in apparent contradiction to other passages which seemingly embrace "dogmatic views" such as *karma* and *saṃsāra*. But, as with the Pyrrhonist texts and those of Nāgārjuna and Candrakīrti, these early Buddhist passages too may be read, I suggest, as performative assertions or caveats calling into question any dogmatic commitment to nonevident beliefs which otherwise seem to be implied in terms as *karma* and *saṃsāra*. Indeed, the hyper-reality implied by these notions is undermined by the transformation they necessarily undergo at the point of liberation; *karma* and *saṃsāra* and other similar notions as we understand them prior to liberation are, in the end, illusions to be dissipated. The point, finally, is *not* to believe in them.[110]

In an extraordinary passage in the *Aṭṭhakavagga*, we get the following conclusion: "'There is a state where form ceases to exist,' said the Buddha. 'It is a state without ordinary perception and without disordered perception and without no perception and without any annihiliation of perception. It is perception, consciousness, that is the source of all the basic obstacles.'"[111] However this complex passage may be read, it seems to suggest that perception in the wake of liberation is neither "ordinary" nor "disordered," but that some kind of perception clearly continues. It is "form," not "perception," which is annihiliated; perception remains, yet it is no longer subject to form, to interpretations dictated by one or another belief, so presumably it can be appreciated for what it is, perhaps in the sense in which appearances can be appreciated for what they are by the Pyrrhonists once judgments about them have been suspended. Of course for most Buddhists, certain physical responses, such as sexual arousal, are widely presented in the texts as desires to be avoided, as if they were not perceptions but beliefs or judgments about perceptions, while by contrast we find no corresponding blanket avoidance of physical responses, including sexual arousal, among the Pyrrhonists; for the latter, sexual arousal appears to be not a judgment, but an appearance, albeit subject, like all appearances, to distorting judgments. It is not clear whether or not this difference points to any fundamental incompatibility between Madhyamaka Buddhism and Pyrrhonism; a deeper common resolution may be possible, but that is not a question which can be pursued here.

—◦◦◦—

So far I have been mapping the common ground between key Pyrrhonist and Buddhist texts, while acknowledging compatible differences in technique and emphasis, as well as a certain ambiguity over some issues—for example, with regard to sexuality—as to what constitutes a perception or appearance on the one hand, and a judgment about perceptions or appearances on the other. It might still be wondered whether there are any clearly incompatible differences between the two traditions. Let me conclude this East-West comparison by considering a recent study by David Burton on Nāgārjuna, *Emptiness Appraised*, which includes a rare comparative assessment of Nāgārjuna and the Greek sceptics. Burton sees serious incompatibilities separating the Greek sceptics from Nāgārjuna and the subsequent Madhyamaka tradition. Burton defines Pyrrhonism as a realization of a conceptual construct he calls "global scepticism"[112] : A global sceptic holds that "(a) {It is not known whether x or ~x} and (b) {it is not known whether or not it can be known whether x or ~x} [where x stands for any matter whatsoever]. Neither (a) nor (b) is a knowledge-claim."[113] Nāgārjuna, it turns out for Burton, fails to meet this standard, even though he claims that he has no views, positions, theses, etc. How does he fail? As Burton puts it:

> When Nāgārjuna says that he does not have a view/position/thesis, this means that he does not have a view/position/thesis which asserts the *svabhāva* [substance] of entities. But Nāgārjuna does uphold the position that entities lack *svabhāva*. Unlike the sceptic, for whom there is no knowledge of phenomena in their real nature, Nāgārjuna contends that there can be knowledge of entities in their real nature. Emptiness is not a doctrine which denies that there is knowledge. Entities as they really are exist without *svabhāva*, and this is knowledge.[114]

Just as Bett concluded that Pyrrho was not a Pyrrhonist, but in fact a dogmatic sceptic, so Burton concludes that Nāgārjuna too was a dogmatic sceptic. Burton's claim that Nāgārjuna holds that "there can be knowledge of entities in their real nature" does not square with Nāgārjuna's disclaimers about such assertions cited above, such as "emptiness is the relinquishing of all views." Burton (like Bett) finds it necessary to discount significant evidence to the contrary to sustain his points. For Pyrrhonist and Madhyamaka texts alike both contain important passages, as we have seen, which clearly urge inquirers not only not to hold beliefs about things, but also not to hold beliefs about beliefs about suspending judgment about beliefs. Such reflexive, self-contradictory statements are not asserted because they are self-contradictory, or absurd, or nonsensical, but because they present or picture, in their very absurdity, the self-defeating nature of the project of belief. They are presented in the way of examples, or demonstrations, in the manner of Zen Koans, perhaps, but not as literal statements about some reality or nonreality. This is not an issue that can be settled by scholarly citations. The question is what attitude to adopt towards those citations, particularly those containing self-contradictory statements about our beliefs, about what we do or do not do about our beliefs. Those for whom contradictions are disqualifications, evidence of incompletion, irrationality, confusion, inauthenticity, etc., will find in such passages little or no value, unless some unambiguous referent can be found or created for them. Absent such a referent, on this view, the presence of self-contradictory passages in these texts can only degrade our evaluation of them, leaving their otherwise interesting insights compromised by the presence of these incongruous, irrational, confusing, perplexing passages which, to make sense, must have some independent referent, or the negation of one, if only we could understand it. But for those for whom contradictions have other, positive uses, as in Pyrrhonism and the Madhyamaka, their presence can not only be explained, but anticipated and welcomed.

It is Burton and Bett, by taking nonindicative statements literally, who reify emptiness, tranquility, etc., and expect the same of Pyrrho or Nāgārjuna. Given this approach, we might well expect some enterprising scholar to take on Sextus Empiricus himself, arguing away the paradoxical nonindicative passages to force Sextus onto the Procrustean bed of dogmatic scepticism, in effect eliminating Pyrrhonism itself! Burton does not challenge the Pyrrhonism of Sextus, or any other figure in the tradition, including Pyrrho, but the arguments he uses against Nāgārjuna can just as easily be used against Sextus, or anyone else. We have seen Bett invoke similar arguments, via Aristocles, against Pyrrho. Insofar as they admit only literal readings as the standard of interpretation for any text, Burton and Bett and other dogmatic scholars render nonliteral textual passages unreadable in advance, except insofar as they are forcefully treated as literal texts. These scholars end up destroying the texts in order to save them. Entranced by the stark fixed trees of Academic scepticism, they miss the flowing Pyrrhonian forest beyond. And, in a paradoxical twist with regard to the Indian-Greek connection, they imply that Pyrrhonism and the Madhyamaka might after all share something in common, namely, a dogmatic scepticism or nihilism from which they can no longer be distinguished.

But if Pyrrhonism and the Madhyamaka were both examples of dogmatic scepticism, it's hard to see what motivation adherents of these schools would have had to make such nonsensical, paradoxical statements about their own procedures, which go far beyond anything necessary to express dogmatic scepticism. Since we can have beliefs about our suspensions of judgment about our beliefs, and since any beliefs are naturally suspect, these too, they reasonably conclude, should be put to the test. Beliefs, after all, are often presented as facts. A Pyrrhonian or Madhyamaka practitioner asks whether such purported facts are actually evident or not, that is, whether they are really facts. If not, the "facts" asserted are judged beliefs, and claims about their status are suspended. This testing of beliefs, their suspension, and the associated outcome of tranquillity, is what separates these thinkers from dogmatists, including those who have come to own the label "sceptic"; it is a process which Pyrrhonism and the Madhyamaka realized cannot be construed literally without self-contradiction. This also explains what all the fuss has been about vis-à-vis their opponents. Far from seeing self-contradiction as a defining mark of incoherence and nonsense, or as some kind of mysterious referent, Pyrrhonism and the Madhyamaka use contradictions of this sort as performative acts that, by their very absurdity, occasion a logic-defying liberation which cannot be characterized in any other way. The infinite regress of spiraling suspensions of belief into suspensions of suspensions of belief, and so on, may or may not be how things "really" are, may or may not be relevant, may or may not matter in any ultimate sense. Until and unless we are persuaded by some belief or other we remain free of belief or attachment; we simply notice that "things" appear this way or that way, and we go about our business, without having to worry about what it all "really" means. Both Pyrrhonism and the Madhyamaka appear to share this sceptical middle path through experience, and to recommend it to us. Whatever differences might be proposed to stand between them would have to be weighed against their common, liberating suspension of judgment.

## NOTES

1. An earlier version of this chapter appeared as "Pyrrhonism and the Madhyamaka," in *Philosophy East and West* 57, no. 4, October 2007, 482–511.

2. Phoenician ships may have made the trade wind run to and from India as early as the time of King Solomon, though the story of their doing so, found in the first book of Kings, was recorded only in the sixth century BCE. Cf. Rhys Carpenter, *Beyond the Pillars of Heracles: The Classical World seen Through the Eyes of Its Discoverers* (New York: Delacourt, 1966), 215–19; a more conservative estimate of Mediterranean-Indian contacts can be found in the entry for "India" in the *Oxford Classical Dictionary*, eds. N. G. L. Hammond and H. H. Scullard (Oxford: Clarendon Press, 1970), 544; long-distance trade of some kind, though, was already a feature of Harappan culture: "The Indus Civilization, or alternatively the Mature Harappan (2500–1900 BC), is a time of cities, developed social classes, craft and career specialists, writing and long-distance trade with Mesopotamia, Central Asia, and even the countries at the mouth of the Red Sea," Gregory L. Possehl, *The Indus Civilization: A Con-*

*temporary Perspective* (Walnut Creek, Calif.: Altamira Press, 2002), 1; a recent, exhaustive survey of possible contacts between the Mediterranean and India in ancient times can be found in Thomas McEville, *The Shape of Ancient Thought: Comparative Studies in Greek and indian Philosophies* (New York: Allworth Press, 2002), ch. 1, 1–22, and throughout.

3. Demetrios Th. Vassiliades, *The Greeks in India: A Survey in Philosophical Understanding* (New Delhi: Munshiram Manoharlal Publishers Pvt. Ltd., 2000), 16.

4. Ibid., 22 et passim.

5. Dirk L. Coupris, Robert Han, and Gerard Naddaf, *Anaximander in Context: New Studies in the Origins of Greek Philosophy* (Albany: State University Press of New York, 2003), 54–55.

6. Vassiliades, *Greeks in India*, 29.

7. Ibid, 29–30.

8. Diogenes Laertius, "Pyrrho," in his *Lives of Eminent Philosophe rs*, vol. 2., trans. R. D. Hicks, Loeb Classical Library (Cambridge, Mass.: Harvard University Press, 2000), (IX, 61), 47.

9. Aenesidemus (first century BCE) is sometimes credited as the founder of the Pyrrhonist tradition as we know it, culminating in Sextus Empiricus in the second century BCE. His development of the modes certainly enhanced the tradition, but he himself claimed Pyrrho as the founder, using his name, and Diogenes Laertius in his life of Timon, *Lives*, vol. 2 (IX, 115–16), 525–27, gives a unbroken genealogy from Pyrrho and Timon through Aenesidemus and down to Sextus Empiricus and beyond, suggesting a continuous tradition.

10. The Buddha's agnosticism is perhaps best presented in "The Shorter Discourse to Malunkyaputta," sutta 63 of *The Middle Length Discourses of the Buddha* [*Majjhima Nikāya*], trans. Bhikkhu Nanamoli and ed. Bhikkhu Bodhi (Boston: Wisdom Publications, 1995), 533–36.

11. Richard Bett, *Pyrrho: His Antecedents and His Legacy,* (Oxford: Oxford University Press, 2000), 178.

12. But see McEville, *The Shape of Ancient Thought*, where he writes: "It seems, finally, that the [Persian] Empire was sufficiently polyglot that communication between Greeks and Indians in Susa or elsewhere would not have been a problem; the Greeks, as a people who produced interpreters, may be presumed to have known Persian, and the Indians, whose language was so close, to have picked it up easily. It is possible that the two groups communicated in Aramaic, but also possible that they spoke Persian to one another" (13).

13. Quoted in Ibid., 16.

14. A. A. Long and D. N. Sedley, *The Hellenistic Philosophers*, vol. 1, translations of the principal sources with philosophical commentary (Cambridge: Cambridge University Press, 1987), 16–18. Long and Sedley rely on the Aristocles passage, which they assert to be "remarkably uncontaminated by the centuries of intervening philosophy, and sufficiently different from later Pyrrhonism to be taken as the stance of Pyrrho and Timon themselves. On this construal Pyrrho's skepticism was not simply the outcome of equally-balanced

and undecidable disagreements between philosophers . . . , but the response to a metaphysical thesis, concerning the nature of things."

15. Bett, *Pyrrho*, 60.

16. Ibid., 39–40.

17. Ibid., 82.

18. Diogenes Laertius, "Pyrrho" ( IX, 103), 515.

19. A dogmatic view of language as either indicative or nonsensical is widespread among commentators on Pyrrho and Pyrrhonism besides Bett. Such a view seems taken for granted by Long and Sedley in their commentary on Pyrrhonism (see note 11 above). See also James Warren, *Epicurus and Democritean Ethics: An Archaeology of Ataraxia* (Cambridge: Cambridge University Press, 2002), 86ff. Warren, like Bett, asserts that "Pyrrho was not a Pyrrhonist," and that it would be "foolhardy to claim that Pyrrho should be read as a Sextan sceptic." Warren's conclusions also seem to come from the presumption that language be either indicative or nonsensical; in any event, he seems to read Aristocles and Sextus accordingly, missing the point the Pyrrho and the Pyrrhonists might have had quite other purposes in mind.

20. Diogenes Laertius, "Pyrrho" (IX, 74), 487.

21. Ibid. (IX, 75), 489.

22. Ibid. (IX, 76), 489–90; see also Sextus Empiricus, *Outlines of Scepticism*, trans. Julia Annas and Jonathan Barnes (Cambridge: Cambridge University Press, 2000) (I, 18–27), 46–52; in a footnote on 94, Annas and Barnes note that "assertoric sentences can be used with non-assertoric force."

23. Bett, *Pyrrho*, 113.

24. Everard Flintoff, "Pyrrho and India," *Phronesis* XXV, no. 2, 1980, 88ff.

25. Ibid., 91.

26. Ibid., 91–93.

27. Ibid., 91.

28. Ibid., 91.

29. Cf. James Warren, *Epicurus and Democritean Ethics*, et passim; Warren argues that *euthymia* as used by Democritus foreshadows *ataraxia*, but he cites no instance of Democritus' use of the latter term at all; he gives no indication that the Pyrrhonist sense of *ataraxia* as a release from *all* beliefs might make it something very different from its interpretation in dogmatic contexts, as in Epicureanism and Stoicism.

30. See note 10 above; cf. also "Brahmajala Sutta: The Supreme Net; What the Teaching is Not," in *The Long Discourses of the Buddha*, trans. of the *Digha Nikāya* by Maurice Walshe (Boston: Wisdom Publications, 1995), 67–90; see also "Atthakavagga: The Chapter of the Eights" in the *Sutta Nipāta*, trans. H. Saddhatissa (London: Curzon Press, 1985), 91–113.

31. Flintoff, "Pyrrho and India," 93.

32. Ibid., 94.

33. Harald Thorsrud, "Ancient Greek Scepticism," in *The Internet Encyclopaedia of Philosophy*, www.utm.edu/research/iep/s/skepanci.htm, accessed June 2003.

34. Flintoff, "Pyrrho and India," 96.

35. Ibid., 101.

36. Hiralal Jain, *Jainism in Buddhist Literature*, http://www.ibiblio.org/jainism/database/BOOK/jainbudh.doc, accessed February 2004; the words *ajñāvāda* and "agnosticism" are vitrually identical etomologically.

37. Flintoff, "Pyrrho and India," 99–100.

38. Diogenes Laertius, "Pyrrho" (IX, 67), 479.

39. Diogenes Laertius, "Anaxarchus," in his *Lives of Eminent Philosophers*, vol. 2., trans. R. D. Hicks, Loeb Classical Library (Cambridge, Mass.: Harvard University Press, 2000) (IX, 59), 473.

40. See, for example, McEvilley, *The Shape of Ancient Thought*, 225–36.

41. Flintoff, "Pyrrho and India," 93.

42. R. J. Hankinson, *The Sceptics* (New York: Routledge, 1995), 64.

43. Ibid., 64.

44. Quoted by Diogenes Laertius, "Pyrrho" (IX, 67), 481.

45. Flintoff, "Pyrrho and India," 89.

46. Plutarch, *The Lives of the Noble Grecians and Romans*, trans. John Dryden, revised by Arthur Hugh Clough (New York: Modern Library, n.d.), 52.

47. Herodotus, *The History*, trans. David Grene (Chicago: University of Chicago Press, 1987), (4.44), 297.

48. Ibid. (3.94), 254.

49. Cf. Carpenter, *Beyond the Pillars of Hercules*, chapter VII, "Seaways to India," 215ff. He traces contact by sea between Sumerian cities and Mohenjo-Daro back to the third millennium BCE.

50. Lionel Casson, *Libraries in the Ancient World* (New Haven, Conn.: Yale University Press, 2001), 28–29.

51. Strabo, *Geography*, trans. Horace Leonard Jones, Loeb Classical Library (Cambridge, Mass.: Harvard University Press, 1966), XV, I, 59, 101.

52. Cf. the entry "Megasthenes," in *The Oxford Classical Dictionary*, eds. N. G. L. Hammond and H. H. Scullard, second ed., 665–66.

53. Cf. Bhadantācariya Buddhaghosa, *The Path of Purification* (*Visuddhimagga*), trans. Bhikkhu Nanamoli (Kandy, Sri Lanka: Buddhist Publication Society, 1991), and Arahant Upatissa, *The Path of Freedom* (*Vimuttimagga*), trans. N. R. M. Ehara, Soma Thera, and Kheminda Thera (Kandy, Sri Lanka, Buddhist Publication Society, 1995).

54. "Hesychast," in the *Catholic Encyclopedia*, http://www.newadvent.org/cathen/07301a.htm, accessed February 2004.

55. Porphyry, "On the Life of Plotinus and the Arrangement of his Works," in Plotinus, *The Enneads*, trans. Stephen MacKenna (London: Penguin Books, 1991), civ.

56. See Thomas McEvilley, *The Shape of Ancient Thought: Comparative Studies in Greek and Indian Philosophies* (see note 2 above), 450–90; McEvilley's discussion is based on an earlier article, "Pyrrhonism and Madhyamaka," *Philosophy East and West* 32, no. 1, January 1982, 3–35.

57. Ibid., 484.

58. Ibid., 492.

59. Ibid., 495.

60. Ibid., 492.

61. With regard to the Pyrrhonists, Diogenes Laertius, as noted in the Introduction to the Loeb edition by Herbert S. Long (Diogenes Laertius, "Pyrrho," xxi), "cites hundred of sources," and "most of these authors come from either the third and second centuries B. C. or the first century A. D.," while according to the Introduction by Jonathan Barnes to the *Outlines of Scepticism*, xvi, "the texts which Sextus copied were written at a period when Stoicism was the dominant philosophy," which is to say, three centuries or more before Sextus' time. With regard to the Madhyamaka, cf. "Proto-Madhyamaka in the Pāli Canon," Luis O. Gomez, *Philosophy East and West* 26, no. 2, April 1976, 137–65, where Gomez traces key aspects of the Madhyamaka tradition initiated by Nāgārjuna back to the earliest texts of the Pāli Canon, particularly the *Attakavagga* of the *Sutta-Nipāta*.

62. Sextus Empiricus, *Outlines of Scepticism* (I,19), 8.

63. Ibid. (I, 8), 4.

64. Candrakīrti, *Madhyamakāvatāra* (*The Entry into the Middle Way*), trans. C. W. Huntington and Geshe Namgyal Wangchen (with commentary), *The Emptiness of Emptiness: An Introduction to Early Indian Mādhyamika* (Honolulu: University of Hawaii Press, 1989), (Epilogue, 3), 196.

65. Ibid. (VI, 68), 165.

66. Ibid., 160.

67. As Sextus puts it: "we argue not against all signs, but only against indicative signs [of nonevident things], which seem to be a fiction of the Dogmatists. For recollective signs are found convincing by everyday life: seeing smoke, someone diagnoses fire; having observed a scar, he says that a wound was inflicted. Hence not only do we not conflict with everyday life, but we actually join the struggle on its side, assenting without opinion to what it has found convincing and taking a stand against the private fictions of the Dogmatists." Sextus Empiricus, *Outlines of Scepticism* (II, 102), 93; an example of the kind of indicative sign used by the dogmatists to go beyond appearances as noted by Sextus is the notion that "bodily movements are signs of the soul," Sextus Empiricus, *Outlines of Scepticism* (II, 101), 93.

68. On the various beliefs built upon sensations and thoughts, cf. Adrian Kuzminski, *The Soul* (New York: Peter Lang Publishing, 1994), 43–85.

69. Diogenes Laertius, "Pyrrho" (IX, 106), 517.

70. Candrakīrti, *Entry into the Middle Way* (VI, 175), 179.

71. C. W. Huntington, Jr., *The Emptiness of Emptiness*, 24–25.

72. Cf. Sextus Empiricus, *Outlines of Scepticism* (I, 227), 60, and Samkara, *The Thousand Teachings* (*Upadesa Sahasri*), trans. A . J. Alston (London: Shanti Sadan, 1990), 87, 165, 194, 268, 292, 329, 336; McEvilley, *The Shape of Ancient Thought*, notes that "Sextus and Nagarjuna use the same exemplum, wood and fire," 462; see also 498.

73. Candrakīrti, *Entry into the Middle Way* (VI, 165), 177.

74. Nāgārjuna, *Mūlamadhyamakakārikā* (*The Fundamental Wisdom of the Middle Way*), trans. Jay L. Garfield (with commentary), *The Fundamental*

*Wisdom of the Middle Way: NĀgĀrjuna's Mūlamūdhyamakakārikā* (New York and Oxford: Oxford University Press, 1995) (XVII, 15), 45.

75. Sextus Empiricus, *Outlines of Scepticism* (I, 14), 6.

76. Ibid. (I, 223), 58.

77. Candrakīrti, *Entry into the Middle Way* (VI, 68), 165.

78. Nāgārjuna, *Fundamental Wisdom* (XXV, 24), 76.

79. Candrakīrti in his *Prasannapadā Mūlamadhymakavṛtti* writes: "For those with deep insight the truth of the highest meaning is a state of silence." Quoted and translated by C. W. Huntington, Jr., "Was Candrakīrti a Prāsaṅgika?" in *The Svātantrika-Prāsaṅgika Distinction: What Difference does a Difference Make?* ed. Georges B. J. Dreyfus and Sara L. McClintock (Boston: Wisdom Publications, 2003), 78.

80. Sextus Empiricus, *Outlines of Scepticism* (I, 20), 48.

81. Cf. C. W. Huntington, Jr., *The Emptiness of Emptiness*, 58, and Sextus Empiricus, *Outlines of Scepticism* (I, 10), 5; (I, 192), 47–48.

82. Candrakīrti, *Entry into the Middle Way* (VI, 185), 180.

83. Nāgārjuna, *Fundamental Wisdom* (XIII, 8), 36.

84. Ibid. (XXII, 11), 61.

85. Ibid. (XV, 10), 40.

86. Ibid. (XVIII, 8), 49.

87. Sextus Empiricus, *Outlines of Scepticism* (I, 192), 47–48.

88. Ibid. (I, 59), 17.

89. Ibid. (I, 206), 52.

90. Diogenes Laertius, "Pyrrho" (IX, 105), 515.

91. Ibid. (IX, 107), 519; also Sextus Empiricus, *Outlines of Pyrrhonism* (I, 29), 21.

92. Sextus Empiricus, *Outlines of Scepticism* (I, 28), 10.

93. Diogenes Laertius, "Pyrrho" (IX, 61), 475.

94. Candrakīrti, *Entry into the Middle Way* (VI, 205), 181.

95. Nāgārjuna, *Fundamental Wisdom* (XXVI, 10), 78.

96. Ibid. (XXV, 19), 75.

97. Diogenes Laertius, "Pyrrho" (IX, 104), 515.

98. Ibid. (IX, 104), 515.

99. Ibid. (IX, 61), 475.

100. Sextus Empiricus, *Outlines of Scepticism* (I, 23), 9.

101. Ibid. (I, 135), 35.

102. Nāgārjuna, *Fundamental Wisdom* (XXIV, 18), 69.

103. Candrakīrti, *Entry into the Middle Way* (VI, 151), 176.

104. Adrian Kuzminski, *The Soul*, 21–42.

105. Cf. Luis O. Gomez, "Proto-Madhyamaka in the Pāli canon," *Philosophy East and West* 25, no. 2, April 1976, 137ff.

106. "Atthakavagga: the Chapter of the Eights," *Sutta-Nipāta*, 92.

107. Ibid. (IV, 5, 5), 95.

108. Ibid. (IV, 11, 9), 102.

109. Ibid. (IV, 11, 11), 102.

110. There are other texts which points to the centrality of suspension of judgment in early Buddhism. Exploring these texts in detail is beyond the scope of this work, but some indication of their importance might be noted. One such text is *The Holy Teaching of Vimalakīrti*, trans. Robert A. F. Thurman (University Park: Pennsylvania State University Press, 1976); in his preface Thurman points out that Nāgārjuna "revived the Mahāyāna traditions, discovering the Mahāyāna Sanskrit Scriptures, the *Vimalakīrti* text among them" (ix); Vimalakīrti is presented as a contemporary of the Buddha, a householder, not a monk, who relies on exploiting contradictions to confute beliefs; Vimalakīrti tells us: "Enlightenment is the annihilation of all convictions. Enlightenment is free from all discriminative constructions. Enlightenment is free from all vacillation, mentation, and agitation. Enlightenment is not involved in any commitments. Enlightenment is the arrival at detachment, through freedom from all habitual attitudes" (35). Other texts along these lines include the *Prajñāpāramitā*, or *Perfection of Wisdom* sutras. To quote just one passage: "This perfection of wisdom cannot be expounded, or learned, or distinguished, or considered, or stated, or reflected upon by means of the *skandhas*, or by mans of the elements, or by means of the sense-fields. This is a consequence of the fact that all dharmas are isolated, absolutely isolated. Nor can the perfection of wisdom be understood otherwise than by the *skandhas*, elements or sense-fields. For just the very *skandhas*, elements and sense-fields are empty, isolated and calmly quiet. It is thus that the perfection of wisdom and the *skandhas*, elements and sense-fields are not two, nor divided. As a result of their emptiness, isolatedness and quietude they cannot be apprehended. The lack of a basis of apprehension in all dharmas, that is called 'perfect wisdom.'" *The Perfection of Wisdom in Eight Thousand Lines and Its Verse Summary*, trans. Edward Conze (San Francisco: City Lights, 2006), 138.

111. "Aṭṭhakavagga: the Chapter of the Eights," *Sutta-Nipāta* (IV, 11, 13), 102.

112. David Burton, *Emptiness Appraised: A Critical Study of Nāgārjuna's Philosophy* (Delhi: Motilal Banarsidass, 1999), 22.

113. Ibid., 23.

114. Ibid., 36–37.

# ③

# The Evident and the Nonevident

Pyrrhonism, like Buddhism, cannot be understood without clarifying what we mean by the "evident" and the "nonevident." Yet clearly distinguishing the evident from the nonevident is a job not easily done. I propose to examine in this chapter more closely the Pyrrhonists' attitude towards what they consider to be evident—those immediate, direct, involuntary experiences they most often call appearances (*phainomena*), that is, our sensations and thoughts—as well as nonevident. In this endeavor, I will continue, in part, the comparative analysis of Pyrrhonist and Buddhist accounts of experience begun in the last chapter. My primary emphasis will be on Pyrrhonism, but I hope to shed some light as well on Buddhist observations concerning the evident and nonevident.

—⁓⁓—

Appearances are not abstractions of some sort for Pyrrhonists, as they are for Platonists, Aristotelians, Stoics, Epicureans, and most of their modern mainstream successors in Western philosophy. All these schools have presumed that postulated abstract entities of some sort—variously described as concepts, forms, categories, essences, etc.— constitute the reality of appearances, which otherwise are no more than changing, fleeting, unstable, chaotic ephemera. As I suggested in chapter 1, in mainstream Western philosophy, ancient and modern, appearances, the most primitive of our cognitions are already presumed to be structured, already presumed to reflect some kind of synthesis of form and content, order and chaos. Pyrrhonists by contrast suspend any such notion of synthesis, and endeavor instead to take appearances at face value. They assert that appearances indeed do have a face value, that is, some kind of reliably distinguishing character immediately and directly manifest to consciousness. They start with such appearances them-selves, rather than with other factors (concepts, forms, etc.) commonly presumed to inform appearances and bring them into realization. Once the form/content, order/chaos dichotomies are suspended, there is no reason to assume that appearances have to be explained; instead they themselves can become the principles of explanation.

This is the "Copernican revolution" of Pyrrhonism with regard to mainstream Western philosophy. To appear (*phainesthai*) in Greek is simply to "shine forth," to become directly manifest, like a light in the darkness. The term literally refers to what we immediately see, but it is also used generally by Sextus to indicate any appearance at all, in-cluding the appearances of the other senses, and even of our thoughts. An appearance, an immediate experience of any sort which "shines forth," can disclose itself only by being somehow differentiated from other appearances, other shining forths: the sight of the blue sky is one appearance, the sound of the owl screeching in the night is another, the smell of a gardenia a third, the memory of my grandmother a fourth, and so on, each one of these standing out precisely insofar as it is not any of the others, but something distinct, with its own integrity.

I offer in this chapter a reading of Sextus on appearances (with fur-ther comparative references to Buddhist sources) that is quite different from the predominately held views in the Western tradition, ancient and modern. In that tradition, to restate the key point, an appearance normally is presumed to be some kind of synthesis of form and con-tent, universality and particularity. The reasoning behind this seems to run as follows: Form as such is empty or abstract; for something de-terminate or concrete to be realized, form has to be given content, and vice-versa. Content fills the form, as it were, with the energy of its constant flux, or activity; it fleshes it out, giving it an internal resist-ance, a sensual or imaginative realization. Order disciplines and fo-cuses the otherwise inchoate content, freezing it, as it were, creating a coherence otherwise lacking. As Kant puts it in a widely quoted for-mulation: "Thoughts without content are empty, intuitions without concepts are blind."[1] Kant's intuition, like the indeterminate matter of Aristotle, is a chaotic energized flux without order. And, as with Aris-totle, only when it is brought together with an abstract conceptual ap-paratus of some sort can something determinate result.[2] Even empiri-cist philosophers from Locke to the positivists, who stipulated impressions or sense data as the elementary building blocks of experi-ence, generally understood them to be form-and-content packages; and this is what most modern philosophers continue to believe about per-ceptions, the modern term for appearances.

This form-content synthesis, so widely presupposed in schools of modern Western philosophy, is not to be found in the Pyrrhonist literature we have, and we have no warrant for reading it into it. Insofar as modern scholars persist in reading the Pyrrhonist texts through the lens of some form-content synthesis, those texts are rendered largely incomprehensible. And it is not surprising that Pyrrhonism, which was taken seriously even if misunderstood by many early modern philosophers—including Pico della Mirandola, Ficino, Montaigne, Gassendi, Descartes, Huet, Foucher, Malbranche, Bayle, Berkeley, and Hume, among others—has become increasingly marginalized in post-Kantian Western philosophy.[3] But if we suspend, as the Pyrrhonists urge us to do, the presupposition that experience is a product of some kind of form-content synthesis, then we shall be in a better position not only to appraise what Sextus and other Pyrrhonists had in mind by appearances, but also to appreciate and take seriously the significance of Pyrrhonism as a viable philosophy. We shall be in a better position as well to compare further the Pyrrhonist understanding of experience with the Madhyamaka, where we also find a determination not to make claims that go beyond what is apparent.

—◦◦◦—

Let us consider, then, what Sextus has to say about what is apparent, or evident. For him, the apparent is the standard or criterion (*kriterion*) of action, the only reasonable criterion one could have, the others all being nonevident dogmatic beliefs of one sort or another. "We say, then," he tells us, "that the standard of the Sceptical [Pyrrhonian] persuasion is what is apparent, implicitly meaning by this the appearances [*phainomenon*]; for they depend on passive and unwilled feelings [*pathei*] and are not objects of investigation."[4] To be an object of investigation is to be somehow nonevident; appearances, however, are presumed evident, to be what they appear to be, no more or less. There is no need for them to be explained away by something else; indeed, they can only be subjects (not objects) of explanation. We can only look at them, as it were, and not behind, or beyond, or within them; we cannot derive them from anything else. Another passage from the *Outlines*, written under the heading, "Do Sceptics reject what is apparent?" tells us more, almost as a warning:

> Those who say that the Sceptics reject what is apparent have not, I think, listened to what we say. As we said before, we do not overturn anything which leads us, without our willing it, to assent in accordance with a passive appearance—and these things are precisely what is apparent. When we investigate whether existing things are such as

they appear, we grant that they appear, and what we investigate is not what is apparent but what is said about what is apparent—and this is different from investigating what is apparent itself. For example, it appears to us that honey sweetens (we concede this inasmuch as we are sweetened in a perceptual way); but whether (as far as the argument goes) it is actually sweet is something we investigate—and this is not what is apparent but something said about what is apparent.[5]

The only criterion Pyrrhonists recognize, Sextus tells us again in *Against the Logicians*, is appearance as such, since it is by appearance that we do certain things, and not others; no other criteria, including any by which certain things are said either to exist or not exist, are needed: "For the sceptical [Pyrrhonian] philosopher, if he is not to be entirely inert and without a share in the activities of daily life, was necessarily obliged to possess some Criterion both of choice and of aversion—that is to say, the Appearance; even as Timon also testified in his saying—'Yes, the Appearance is ev'rywhere strong, where'er it approacheth.'"[6]

What is apparent is stated to be anything that we experience *involuntarily*, with which we must "go along." Sextus speaks of following along with appearances "as a boy is said to go along with his chaperon," a situation in which one finds oneself neither embracing nor rejecting the experience, but "yielding without adherence."[7] And further, he says that "an appearance, then, will actually be of the feeling [*pathe*] of a sense—and that is different from an external existing object."[8] The Greek *pathos* has the primary sense of one's being subject to an experience, of enduring a change one cannot evade, in the sense of not being able not to feel it, not to be able to resist the alteration in consciousness that *is* the appearance. We think of "feelings" as emotional states, but *pathos* has a deeper sense of involuntary imposition of any sort, what Timon seems to have meant by saying appearance is "everywhere strong." Appearances understood as "feelings" are not to be construed here as separate or secondary experiences that somehow accompany our immediate experiences, as the feeling of fear might be said to accompany the sight of a snake. The fear of the snake is a complete and independent feeling in itself for the Pyrrhonist, no less so than the sight of the snake, also a complete and independent feeling, but a separate one. Indeed, the test is that they can be separated. It is possible to experience fear in no way connected with snakes, and also to experience snakes without fear. In modern culture we tend to distinguish between emotionally charged internal or subjective feelings and cognitively neutral or objective appearances supposedly caused by outside stimuli, as if they were two different things. Pyrrhonists make no such distinction; appearances *are* feelings, not their purported causes; the notion of inside vs. outside is irrelevant.

Sextus usually reserves the terms *phainomenon* and *aestheton* for a sensory appearance and *noomenon* and *noeton* for a thought appearance, but they are all feelings, or *pathos*, understanding by that the involuntarily evident objects of consciousness. An "object" here is anything determinate enough in some sense to be distinguished from other "objects." We should think of objects not as abstract concepts, such as substances, forms, matter, etc., but rather as distinct albeit sometimes amorphous *pathai* like the sight of a tree, the taste of orange-flavored chocolate, or the dread that follows rejection. These even an infant, not yet structured into his or her culture's modes of interpretation, can experience. All objects of consciousness for the Pyrrhonists are equally involuntary. I can no more not see the blue sky on a sunny afternoon outside, if my eyes are working, than I cannot imagine, if my mind is working, my grandmother if someone speaks her name. Neither the blue sky so seen nor my grandmother so recalled are any kind of form-content synthesis in the Pyrrhonists' view. They are just what they are, not to be distinguished by any extraneous or separate criterion, and they come to us involuntarily and self-differentiated as ready-made complexes, mutually defined in contrast to one another. Appearances constitute a reality, or a network of realities, in which we seem to be embedded; they resist, under the questioning of the Pyrrhonists, at least so far, resolution into any other reality. Pyrrhonists see no reason (yet) to distinguish between appearance and reality. Indeed, appearance appears as its own reality, provided we accept it just as the peculiar reality that it is: immediately, directly, involuntarily, interdependently, and yet unconditionally evident to us, at least, at once both enduring and changing, no more and no less. But if we seek to explain appearance as a function of some form-content synthesis, or anything else, then it becomes mere appearance, a secondary function of more basic factors, of other criteria, which are themselves beyond appearances as such, and so necessarily nonevident. Form apart from content can no more be an appearance for Pyrrhonists than content apart from form; both remain, it seems, equally nonevident. More important, for Pyrrhonists there is no reason to derive appearances from form and content, or anything else.

—⟊⟊⟊—

What more can a Pyrrhonist say about appearances? We have noted Sextus' emphasis on the involuntary or passive nature of appearances. We have also noted that for Pyrrhonists appearances are immediate objects of experience, that is, of consciousness. And as we have noted in previous chapters, these objects, which exist interdependently (the Buddhist would say they are dependently originated) include not only our sensations, that is, our sights, sounds, touches, tastes, and smells, but also our thoughts. Since the Pyrrhonist-Buddhist approach here on sensations and thoughts is so at odds with widely accepted Western views of body and mind, it is worth exploring it in some detail. In the West mind and body are widely understood as the polar opposites that sum up and exhaust our experience, the former widely identified with reality and the latter with appearance. In Pyrrhonism and Buddhism they are both understood to be appearances, each evident and real in their own ways, but they are not exhaustive; together they are contrasted with something else real in its own way, their negation, the emptiness of what is nonevident. We shall return to the emptiness of the nonevident below, but first some more about thoughts and sensations.

Here Sextus includes thoughts along with sensations as appearances:

> just as the things seen are called visible because of the fact that they are seen, and the audible terms audible because of the fact that they are heard, and we do not reject the visible things because they are not heard, nor dismiss the audible things because they are not seen (for each object ought to be judged by its own special sense and not by another), so also the things thought [phronoumena] will exist, even if they should not be viewed by the sight or heard by the hearing because they are perceived by their own proper criterion.[9]

In another passage, he puts it this way:

> For a Sceptic [Pyrrhonist] is not, I think, barred from having thoughts, if they arise from things which give him a passive impression and appear evidently to him and do not at all imply the reality of what is being thought of—for we can think, as they say, not only of real things, but also of unreal things. Hence someone who suspends judgment maintains his sceptical condition while investigating and thinking; for it has been made clear that he assents to any impression given by way of a passive appearance insofar as it appears to him.[10]

Annas and Barnes, in translating this last passage, have Sextus telling us that our thoughts "arise" from our passive impressions, or appearances, as if one sort of thing, our thoughts, were caused by another sort, our appearances. But the verb (hypopiptontoon), literally to "fall under," has as a further meaning, "to get in under, or among," suggesting not a causal or dependent relation between different sorts of things, but a grouping among or within one sort. In other words, we can read Sextus here as telling us that thoughts are to be found nowhere except among appearances, that they too are passive appearances to which we must give assent just as much as sights, sounds, etc., no more and no less so. As Sextus makes clear, to suspend judgment is not to suspend thinking, for we continue to have thoughts—just as we continue to have sensations—even though judgments about each are suspended.

Only if thoughts were somehow objects that were not appearances, as understood by Pyrrhonists, would their status need to be explained. Sextus, however, leaves no room in his texts for anything other than evident appearances on the one hand, and beliefs in nonevident things on the other. That he nowhere addresses this point suggests that it is not an issue for him; his observation (consistent with the overall Pyrrhonist attitude) is that thoughts, as a factual matter, are to be included among appearances, as another dimension, as the sixth sense, as it were. Although Sextus offers relatively little by way of comparison between these two sorts of appearances, sensations and thoughts, a passage in *Against the Professors*, is helpful. Here is the Loeb Library translation by R. G. Bury:

> In general, also, everything conceived is conceived in two main ways, either by way of clear impression or by way of transference from things clear, and this [latter] way is threefold,—by similarity, or by composition, or by analogy. Thus, by clear impression are conceived the white, the black, the sweet and the bitter, and by transference from things clear are concepts [*noeitai*] due to similarity,—such as Socrates himself from a likeness of Socrates, and those due to composition,—such as the hippocentaur from horse and man, for by mixing the limbs of horse and man we have imagined the hippocentaur which is neither man nor horse but a compound of both. And a thing is conceived by way of analogy also in two ways, sometimes by way of increase, sometimes by decrease; for instance from ordinary men— "such mortals as now we see"—we conceived by way of increase the Cyclops who was "Less like a corn-eating man than a forest-clad peak of the mountains;" and by decrease we conceive the pygmy whom we have not perceived through sense-impressions.[11]

The Greek phrase in the first sentence of this passage, translated by Bury as "everything conceived is conceived," is *pan to nooumenon*, literally "all the thoughts." The modern sense of "conception" as some kind of abstract cognitive process is foreign to the text, which speaks simply of "thoughts" as mental images, as the examples of Socrates, the hippocentaur, the Cyclops, etc., make plain. These are directly experienced as things manifest [*enarge*]. We can read Sextus this way: We take certain appearances we have ready to hand, principally our thoughts or imaginings, and substitute them for other appearances not so ready to hand; thus we substitute the appearance of the likeness of Socrates (our mental image of the bald, snub-nosed man) for the visual, audible, etc., appearance of Socrates, which we might have of him if we met him in the street. And so on for images we can compound from others not compounded, and those that are analogous to but distinct from those to which they are analogous (smaller, say, or larger, etc.). Now a sensible appearance, like a statue or portrait of Socrates, can be used as a representation of the physical Socrates just as much as a mental image or thought of him; but it is the virtual effortlessness of our imaginative projections which allows the free and easy substitution of thoughts for almost any other appearances. It is much easier simply to "think" of Socrates, or Santa Claus, or any other physical thing, than it is to describe it in words, or draw a picture of it. The large and seemingly effortless capacity of thought, and its ease of use in substituting for other appearances (signing), may be the principal distinguishing feature of human beings, compared to other animals.

The Buddhist observations corresponding to what Sextus calls "appearances" are the aggregates (*skandhas*). There are five of these: *rūpa*, or form, which has the sense of an involuntary experience, one which offers resistance of some sort; *vedana*, or feeling, the immediate sensation or presence of an object of experience; *saṃjñā*, or our mediate sensations, perceptions, and cognitions, that is, the patterning of connections and associations among objects; *saṃskāra*, or attachments or beliefs about objects; and *vijñāna*, or consciousness. Although this inventory of experience is organized differently from what we find in the Pyrrhonist texts, we find in both cases a compatible summary of characteristics of objects of consciousness on the one hand, and consciousness on the other. The *skandhas* as such are compatible with the six senses, plus consciousness itself as the non-object, or subject, of those senses.[12] The objects and subjects of consciousness in evident both cases, though, as we shall see below, objects are evident in a different way than subjects. And we shall also see that Pyrrhonists adopt this same view of consciousness also being evident, albeit in a different way. The fact that we have beliefs is also evident enough in Buddhism as well as Pyrrhonism, and the objects of our beliefs are similarly not evident. In the Buddhist, and particularly Madhyamaka texts, appearances, or the objects of consciousness, are said to be "empty," as we have seen, without any kind of underlying, explanatory or supporting substance; they are defined instead by their mutual internal and external relations, by what the Buddhists call "dependent origination." We shall explore some of these parallels more fully below.

———~~~———

Sextus makes clear in numerous passages that the appearances he discusses are always *his* appearances. But he also tells us in the *Outlines* that "what is apparent appears to everyone in the same way."[13] In *Against the Logicians*, he elaborates the point:

> For every sensible thing ought naturally to present itself alike to all who are in a like condition and be similarly apprehended. Take white colour, for instance: it is not apprehended in one way by Greeks, in another by barbarians; or in a special way by craftsmen and differently by ordinary folk; but in one and the same way by all those who have their senses unimpeded. Bitter and sweet, again, are not tasted in this way by this man and in a different way by that man, but similarly by each of those who are in a similar condition.[14]

How can appearances be at once private and public? Pyrrhonism, like Buddhism, steers a "middle path," avoiding solipsism on the one hand and behaviorism on the other. I cannot see that you see the same sight I see (say, a snake), for I can see it only through my eyes, not yours. I can see that your body reacts as does mine (we both recoil), so I see, whatever appearance you may have privately, that we, or at least our bodies, react "in the same way" to what I at least see. This does not yet show that what is apparent "appears to everyone in the same way." I might, however, query you about what you saw, and you might describe it to me, or perhaps even draw me a picture. Your representation of what you saw (your narrative or picture) provides me with an appearance of an appearance. And here I have something evident to go by. Should it match the appearance I experienced, that is, accurately and consistently represent it, then I can fairly conclude that you and I shared the same appearance. If it fails to match, then I can fairly conclude that we did not share the same appearance. If it matches in some respects but not in others, I can conclude only that we shared perhaps similar appearances, but not necessarily the same one.

Each of us can produce for the other appearances we each recognize privately. To do this is to do no more or less than use one appearance as a sign for another, associating two appearances not normally associated. When we learn the alphabet, for instance, the teacher speaks the sound of the audible letter while writing the corresponding visible letter on the blackboard, or displaying it on a computer screen.

Through consistent experience, we learn to associate the two, though nothing about the audible and visual letters in themselves suggests any particular association. Indeed, their association is an arbitrary one. As a child, I come to see and hear and associate what my teacher sees and hears and associates in writing and reciting to me the alphabet, and discover that I can do the same myself. I learn to write and recite the alphabet myself, and then I am in a position to teach it to someone else, and so on. Similarly, I can see your finger pointing to a circle drawn on the blackboard as well as my finger pointing to the same circle, although I see them as I see them, not as you see them. But I can see that my visual field includes your finger as well as mine, and that your finger behaves like mine, so that I accept the gesture you indicate to me ("this is what I see") since it is the kind of gesture I can indicate to you. Since I can bring my own attention to the circle on the blackboard by pointing to it using my finger, when I see a finger not my own pointing to it in the same way, I can reliably conclude that you and I are sharing at least a similar appearances on a circle on the blackboard.

The classic nihilist objection to this line of observation is "How do you know you aren't being fooled?" You might be no more than a brain in a vat, hallucinating appearances that you believe are shared by others, but which are yours alone. This is an argument that must be stood on its head. Why should we doubt that we share appearances? Wittgenstein argues cogently in *On Certainty* that "the game of doubt itself presupposes certainty."[15] The argument that we can doubt all or any experience presupposes the dual belief (1) that experience (composed of appearances) is entirely subjective, and (2) that the job of such appearance is nonetheless to represent an objective world. This is impossible, modern sceptics point out, and they appeal to various perceptual illusions (of which the "oar straight in air but bent in water" is a stock example) to make their point. But why anyone should accept these assumptions, we are not told. We are told we cannot trust our senses because they can be unreliable and unpredictable, and that we must therefore discount them in favor of the belief that if there are reliable entities they must be other than appearances. But, as Pyrrhonists point out, there are no illusions of appearances as such, appearances simply being what they are. What we can have, however, is a contradiction between one set of appearances ("the oar straight in air but bent in water") and some interpretation or view or theory we might have *about* that set of appearances (our expectation or inference that the oar straight in air also ought be straight in water).

If objects of consciousness constitute their own criterion of existence, as Pyrrhonist's propose, they are entirely trustworthy. There can be no mistakes in objects of consciousness, only mistakes about them. To quote Sextus again: "what we investigate is not what is apparent but what is said about what is apparent."[16] In the case of illusions, hallucinations, and other anomalous objects of experience, there is no mistake about them as such. I might see a mirage in the desert. There is no mistaking the mirage itself, that is, the visual experience of a shimmering blur off at a distance. The mistake is to take that blur for a body of water. I might eat a mushroom and watch the trees in the forest dance the tango. There is no mistaking the dancing trees I see. The mistake is to take them for the trees in the forest I saw earlier, that is, for linking them together in terms of some continuous, eternal, substance underlying both. Whenever an anomaly arises among objects of consciousness, it is a clue that we are making mistaken assumptions *about* the objects in question. If the Pyrrhonists are correct and perceptual illusions are in fact illusions of interpretation and not of perception (appearance), then we have no reason to doubt the phenomena we encounter. And no longer need to assume that the phenomena are somehow subjective. Nor is there any good reason, in their view, to doubt that the appearances I entertain can be entertained by you as well.

Indeed, anomalies among objects of consciousness are perhaps the chief clues leading us to question our nonevident assumptions about experience. As nonevident assumptions are suspended, the less apparent are sifted out, it seems, in favor of the more apparent. The Micholson-Morley experiment of 1887, to take a classic example from the history of science, sought to confirm anticipated changes in the speed of light given the assumption that light waves, like waves in water, need a medium through which to travel, what was then called the "luminiferous ether," a nonevident cosmic medium postulated by nineteenth-century physicists. Such a medium, if it existed, was presumed like other mediums to have an effect on the objects moving though it, so that variations in the speed of light waves moving through the ether in different ways might be expected. When Micholson and Morley carried out their famous experiment hoping to measure such differences in the speed of light, they found to their astonishment that no such differences could be detected, that the speed of light appeared to be a constant. Postclassical physics took this anomaly seriously and eventually abandoned the nonevident notion of the luminiferous ether in favor of the evident constancy of the speed of light in relativity theory. For Pyrrhonian sceptics, science is no more or less than the determination of correlations among appearances, that is, what is evident, or can be made so. Science is at one with ordinary life in observing and appreciating such correlations; it differs only in seeking to rule out such nonobservable, nonevident beliefs as distort and confuse our understanding of experience.

Science, however, is also a source of dogmatism, as the Pyrrhonists made plain. Having observed certain regularities of nature displayed by otherwise seemingly unstable appearances, many scientists, ancient and modern, have leapt to the conclusion that this patterning, the forms displayed by changing phenomena, constitutes the essence of things, the criterion of their existence, perhaps even some kind of "intelligent design." Sextus offers us one account of this leap of faith by scientists who embraced a controlling belief in nonevident reason [logos]:

> it is held that the Physicists, from Thales down, were the first to introduce the inquiry regarding the criterion. For when they had condemned sensation as being in many cases untrustworthy, they set up reason as the judge of the truth [ton logon kriten] in existing things, and starting out from this they arranged their doctrines of principles and elements and the rest, the apprehension of which is gained by means of the faculty of reason. Hence the greatest of the Physicists, Anaxagoras, in disparaging the senses on the ground of their weakness, says, "Owing to their infirmity we are unable to judge what is true." . . . Anaxagoras, accordingly, declared that reason in general is the criterion.[17]

The idea that the senses in particular are untrustworthy is cited by Sextus as the motivation for the dogmatic move by the physicists, a move carried forward by the philosophers, and still a staple of modern thinking. The senses are untrustworthy, it is often said, because we cannot judge on their basis "what is true," whereas reason can reveal the truth behind things. Reason (logos) is a term notoriously rich in range and nuance, but its root meaning is that of "word," or speech, or language, that is, the public expression of private thought. The words we put together in a speech or account or narrative of some sort are presumed to express not appearances as such but some kind of pattern or correlation we can see displayed either among our sensations or our thoughts. The illusion then arises that we can separate and fix the pattern so displayed apart from the instances in which it is displayed, and so make the pattern into an independently existing, everlasting criterion for just what those instances should be. The pattern, at least, appears pure and unchanging, insulated from corruption, an object perhaps worthy of attachment, but, if considered separate from sensations and thoughts, necessarily a belief in something nonevident, a myth or an ideology. The fear naturally aroused by the uncertainty of change, and by knowing our own mortality, is perhaps all the motivation necessary to embrace a myth like reason, or *logos*, which promises a world of enduring entities immune from change and dissolution.

Experience for the Pyrrhonist, by contrast, consists in precisely what the dogmatists distrust and fear: the myriad of more or less patterned appearances, appearing and disappearing, representing and contrasting with one another; sometimes highly correlated, and at other times less so, or not at all. Objects of consciousness simultaneously exhibit permanence and change insofar as they endure or fail to endure in consciousness. Many objects of consciousness reliably recur: the book I pick up on my desk seems to be the same book I left there yesterday; a mental image of my grandmother I have today seems to be the same mental image I had of her yesterday; and so on, it seems, for virtually any appearance. And of course I also can pick up a similar but different book, or have a similar but different image of my grandmother. And even dissimilar things are often consistently correlated in our experience. The appearance of an object, consistently correlated with another (even if dissimilar), thereby comes to signify its correlate. I hear the sound of an automobile passing outside without seeing it, but I assume that I could see it if I looked out the window. I have only the audible automobile in consciousness, at the moment, while the visible automobile remains nonevident. But the consistency of correlation of sounds and sights of just this type justifies the expectation of being able (if I look out the window) to experience the visual automobile as well. In contrast to the dogmatic traditions, knowledge for the Pyrrhonists turns out to be knowledge of what is evident or likely to be so, knowledge of the objects of consciousness, of appearances, just as they appear in consciousness, including their various correlations, and no more or less. Far from doubting knowledge, the Pyrrhonists doubt only claims to knowledge of nonevident things, of things that seem unable to appear as objects of consciousness. If objects of consciousness constitute their own criterion of existence, as Pyrrhonists propose, they are entirely trustworthy and unproblematically knowable. They are not subjective or objective, or reducible, it seems, to any terms other than their own.

Madhyamaka Buddhists, like the Pyrrhonists, doubt claims to knowledge of nonevident things and accept the reality of what is evident, such as it is: interdependent and subject to change. Nāgārjuna tells us that "Everything is real and is not real, both real and not real, neither real nor not real. This is the Lord Buddha's teaching."[18] In a commentary on this passage, Jay Garfield writes: "This is the positive tetralemma regarding existence. Everything is conventionally real.

Everything is ultimately unreal (that is, not unreal in just any sense, but unreal when seen from the ultimate standpoint). Everything has both characteristics—that is, everything is both conventionally real and ultimately unreal. Nothing is ultimately real or completely non-existent. That is, everything is neither real in one sense nor not-real in another sense."[19] Evident things or appearances, in brief, enjoy conventional reality. They have no independent existence as far as the Madhyamaka is concerned, as we saw in the last chapter, apart from the parts that make them up and the wholes in which they are themselves parts, which are similarly conditioned. But they do have this phenomenal existence, ever subject to changes in circumstances, but nonetheless compelling enough in its involuntary immediacy and reliable enough to constitute a guide to everyday life. The mutual dependency or dependent origination of phenomenal experience is another way of saying that "empty" phenomena constitute their own criterion, without recourse or appeal to any sort of independently existing essence. Although the Buddhist texts commonly speak of the fleetingness of the *skandhas*, which are subject to continual change, this point is stressed, it seems, to demonstrate their "emptiness," their lack of essence, not, as in the mainstream Western tradition, their unreliability. Unlike mainstream Western thought but like Pyrrhonism, the Madhyamaka has no quarrel with evident phenomena as such; indeed Nāgārjuna famously concludes that the *saṃsāra* of the *skandhas* is in the end identical with *nirvāṇa*: "There is not the slightest difference between cyclic existence and *nirvāṇa*. There is not the slightest difference between *nirvāṇa* and cyclic existence."[20]

—✺—

Reading Sextus Empiricus (or Nāgārjuna) can be an elusive and frustrating experience if one hopes to discover some kind of discrete Pyrrhonist (or Madhyamaka) account of things, of what is evident and nonevident. By the nature of both Pyrrhonism and the Madhyamaka and Mahāyāna Buddhist schools generally, no such account is to be had. The open, changing multiplicity of evident appearances, as it seems, along with their resistance to explanation in any terms except their own, rules out any kind of definition of appearances beyond the conventional roster of the six "senses." At best we can get a kind of incomplete inventory of what sorts of things seem evident, and a similarly incomplete list of various dogmatic claims. This lack of closure, or indeterminacy, is characteristic of Sextus' work. The surviving books by Sextus apart from the *Outlines—Against the Logicians, Against the Physicists, Against the Ethicists,* and *Against the Professors*—all have a kind of loose organization; what structure they have is provided mainly by the views of the various dogmatists Sextus confronts. The arguments are varied and somewhat discontinuous, though compatible, with little cumulative progression overall. The works read as informal monologues or lectures, presumably given to students. There is some repetition of material, recycling of examples, and so on, with some topics more or less arbitrarily following others, often introduced with a kind of stylistic invocation starting with some dogmatic claim, X, followed by the formula that if X, then A or B, and since neither A nor B, then no evidence for X, following by a suspension of judgment.

A typical example of this argumentative indeterminacy from *Against the Logicians*—where we see sensations and thoughts further analyzed—runs as follows:

> For if Man discovers the truth, he discovers it by employing either the senses only or the intellect or the combination of both the senses and the intellect; but, as we shall establish, he cannot discover the truth by employing either the senses only or the intellect by itself or both the senses and the intellect conjointly; therefore Man is not capable of discovering the truth. Now he is not able to grasp the truth by the senses alone. . . . For they are by nature irrational [not being explained by anything else], and having no further capacity beyond that of being impressed by the objects imaged, they are wholly disqualified for discovering the truth. For that which is to perceive what is true in the real objects [i.e., beyond appearances] must not only be moved by a whitish or sweetish feeling but also must be brought to have an impression regarding such an object that "this thing is white" and "this thing is sweet." And similarly with the rest of the senses. But to perceive an object of that kind is no longer the task of sense; for sense is of a nature to grasp only colour and flavour and sound, whereas the recognition that "this is white" or "this is sweet," being neither colour nor flavour, is incapable of being experienced by sense.[21]

The "truth" in this passage refers to the nonevident reality postulated by dogmatists to explain our appearances. After some further discussion about the inability of the senses to "discover the truth," Sextus goes on to assess the claim made for the intellect to do the same, and there he offers the following:

> And just as he who does not know Socrates but is looking at the likeness of Socrates does not know whether Socrates resembles the apparent likeness, so the intellect, when it perceives the affections without having discerned the external objects, will not know either the nature of these objects or whether they resemble the affections. And not knowing the apparent things, neither will it understand the

non-evident things which are assumed to be known by transition therefrom.[22]

As far as appearances go, then, we see again that they fall into two broad evident groups, sensations and thoughts, and we come back with Sextus again and again to the point that our knowledge extends no further than to what is evident and therefore not in dispute. Sextus strives again and again to disestablish any kind of postulated non-evident continuity among, beyond, behind, within, or otherwise apart from appearances themselves, leaving the question indeterminate. Even the most stable and concrete of objects, say a rock in the pasture, is no more than a collection of changing sights (now bright, now shaded, now dark), touches (now warm, now cool), and other correlated appearances. That these are consistently and reliably patterned together so that we can expect what we call the "rock" to be there tomorrow, as it has been there as long as anyone remembers, gives the pattern itself no independent right of existence.

But what human beings can do more or less uniquely among sentient beings, it seems, is use some evident appearances to remind themselves of others that are at least temporarily nonevident. Unlike animals, it seems, we can freely, even profusely, project signs about things temporarily nonevident. Only if I am able to do this for myself can I recognize it when others do it, and on that basis I presume (or have no reason not to presume) that there are other selves, albeit that they are as indeterminate and evidently nonevident to themselves as I am to myself. There is nothing specific required for me to believe about other selves, nor about myself. Although each self seems wholly a private perceiver, there is nothing solipsistic about Pyrrhonism. Solipsism is a dogmatic belief, an expression of negative or Academic scepticism that affirms the existence of one's own self, but holds the nonevident belief that no other selves exist. Other selves, it seems, are not evidently nonevident to one as is one's own self, and this is the opening seized by the solipsist. But it does not follow that there are no other selves, only that they are not in any way evident to us. Indeed we should expect that they would be evidently nonevident only to themselves, just as we seem to be evidently nonevident only to ourselves. We will return below to this notion of the evidently nonevident, and how it might be understood; but first we need to clarify further how it is that Pyrrhonists can hold that we can and do share experiences.

Is it enough to show by examining appearances of appearances that we share an appearance? It would appear so. You might be lying to me, but you could lie with confidence only if you already knew what had appeared to me. Of course, you might by chance hit upon the image of a snake and so match the appearance I see, but a chance hit is no more than a coincidence, a random exception, not a rule on which we can rely. A series of repeated, double-blind experiments could be designed to eliminate these possibilities. The burden of proof in any event is not on the Pyrrhonist any longer, but on anyone who would question the reliance on an appearance of an appearance. For the objection presumes something even more problematic, namely, the promise that some external nonevident justification can be produced to establish that one appearance can represent another. The Pyrrhonist reply is that no such justification is needed or desired, or even possible, that appearances come in great variety, and that some of them are identical to one another, others similar to one another (partly identical and partly not), and still others entirely nonidentical or contingent to one another (with no mutual representational value).[23] Two coins I put on a counter may appear to be entirely indistinguishable, that is, identical; if someone switched each one to the location of the other while my back was turned, I could not tell so when I looked at them again. No more is needed to establish identity. The fact that they can be shown to be numerically distinct though otherwise indistinguishable suggests, Pyrrhonists argue, that numerical singularity may *not* be a criterion of identity. Identity, the strongest expression of representation, seems manifest in this way among appearances, as is the weaker representational value we call similarity. If one of the two coins is clipped or dented, the two would only be similar, and I would have no trouble distinguishing them. And if I compare a single visual coin on the counter with the phrase "twenty-five cents," I seem to find between them no representational value whatsoever, only two mutually heterogeneous appearances.

For the Pyrrhonists, comparative values like identity and contrast are simply part and parcel of appearances as such, and need no further explanation. For most dogmatists, the validity of appearances depends on whether or not they truly represent to us the external objects (or forms) which dogmatists presume to be their causes or essences. But this presumption is as unnecessary as it is incoherent. As Sextus puts it, using examples of eggs and snakes rather than coins:

> If, for example, of two eggs that are exactly alike I offer each one in turn to the Stoic for him to distinguish between them, will the [Stoic] Sage be able on inspection to declare indubitably whether the egg exhibited is this one or that other one? And the same argument holds

good in the case of twins. For the Good Man will receive a false presentation, though he has that presentation "imprinted and impressed both by a real object and according to that very object" [what the Stoics called an "apprehensive presentation"], if the presentation he gets be one of Castor as though it were of Polydeuces. . . . [and] when a snake has thrust out its head, if we wish to examine the real object we shall be plunged into great perplexity and shall not be able to say whether it is the same snake that thrust its head out before or another one, as there are many snakes coiled up in the same hole. So then the apprehensive presentation possesses no characteristic whereby it differs from the false and non-apprehensive presentations.[24]

If we insist with the Pyrrhonists that appearances (that is, unmediated or direct, involuntary objects of consciousness, including both sensations and thoughts) be taken as their own criterion, that they be explained in their own terms (that is, in terms of what we agree is evident rather than what is nonevident), an intriguing picture of experience emerges. Objects of consciousness appear to us clustered in heterogeneous groups, our so-called six senses: visual objects, audible objects, tactile objects, gustatory objects, olfactory objects, and thought objects. This heterogeneity is perhaps best expressed by observing something stressed repeatedly by Sextus but overlooked by most of his commentators, namely, that we cannot see what we can hear, touch, taste, smell, and think; nor can we hear what we can see, touch, taste, smell, and think; nor can we touch what we can see, hear, taste, smell, and think; and so on for small, taste, and thought.[25] An apple is a stock example. We can see it, touch it, taste it, hear it, smell it, and think it, but the visible apple as visible differs entirely from the tactile apple as tactile, and so on down the line. Anyone lacking any one of these "senses" could not infer it from the experience of the others, nor of anything else anyone can think of, it seems. Someone born blind can be told about sight, but without experiencing sight a blind person could have no knowledge of it whatsoever, and similarly for the other "senses," including thought.[26]

The dogmatic presumption is that the apple we see is the same apple as the apple we touch, and so on, down to the apple we think. But this sameness is not evident insofar as these appearances have nothing in common as appearances, only that they appear together, that they are consistently correlated. There is no appearance of any commonality as such. All that is evident seems to be that the visual, tactile, auditory, etc., apples are all consistently correlated in our experience. The apple is no more, as Bishop Berkeley wrote centuries later, rehearsing Pyrrhonian arguments, than a bundle of perceptions: "Thus, for example," as Berkeley tells us, "a certain color, taste, smell, figure, and consistence having been observed to go together, are accounted one distinct thing signified by the name 'apple;' other collections of ideas [Berkeley's word for objects of consciousness, that is, appearances] constitute a stone, a tree, a book, and the like sensible things—which as they are pleasing or disagreeable excite the passions of love, hatred, joy, grief, and so forth."[27]

Although the apple I see is consistently correlated with the apple I touch, and with the apple I taste, smell, hear (if I tap it), and think (if I imagine it), there is no common quality I can observe, it seems, in which all these modes of sensation adhere, no underlying substance or Platonic form of "apple." There is no hidden form or category or essence underlying sight and touch and other modes of appearance, no entity that can be construed as what they "really" are. At least no such thing has yet been found actually to appear, that is, to be made evident. It is true that in heterogeneous senses, such as sight and sound, similar and even identical patterns can be displayed. The musical score in my lap I follow with my eyes at a concert in very specific ways matches exactly the sound of the music I hear. A certain arrangement of written notes on the musical staffs corresponds in a remarkable way to a certain arrangement of audible notes stuck by the players on their instruments. Similarly, the words I read in a prepared text at a lecture, if I have the right text, correspond in an equally remarkable way to the words spoken by the speaker at the podium who reads out his lecture. In such cases it would seem that the same pattern is being produced in heterogeneous, entirely different modes—sight and sound. Does this pattern repetition in heterogeneous modes justify the dogmatist's contention that the pattern itself, and patterns like it, constitute some kind of reality behind the appearances which display it, one which we can extract by some kind of process of abstraction? The Pyrrhonist reply is that that such patterns have no apparent existence apart from their display by the various senses, including thoughts, and that no claim beyond correlation of the various senses can be vindicated or is even necessary. We can only see, hear, touch, etc., the pattern in question. There is no exclusive venue for the pattern as such, apart from the various modes of sensation that display it. It simply does not independently appear as itself, as an appearance among other appearances.

The presumption of invariant nonevident abstractions or "primary qualities" underlying our appearances, and existing independently of them—whether called variously forms, essences, categories, "pure" intuitions, concepts, etc.—is a belief in the independent existence of these nonevident objects. Perhaps no other dogmatic belief receives such sustained criticism in Sextus' work, and indeed the ever-shocking doubt of the independent existence of the external world is perhaps the Pyrrhonist's most notorious observation. The Pyrrhonists suspend judgment because they can find nothing evident, that is, no object of consciousness, which fulfills the claim that our purportedly internal appearances actually represent externally existing objects that constitute their true reality. Moreover, they point out this lack of evidence for the external existence of the objects we experience is also a lack of evidence for their internal existence. External and internal are mutually dependent notions of the sort Sextus is fond of pointing out; neither can make sense without the other. To doubt the external world is not to lock ourselves into a subjective prison of appearances, as do Academic and modern sceptics, for there is no warrant either to conclude that our appearances are for each of us alone, even though our experience of them remains private, not public or communal. We have already seen how we can indicate that we share, if not directly certain appearances, then at least some appearances of those appearances, quite enough to confirm to one another publicly that our private experience can also be the private experience of others.

On the Buddhist side, it was left to the Yogācāra school, following the Madhyamaka, to draw the explicit conclusion that we ought not to presume that objects exist independently of our perception of them. Concerned that the Madhyamaka insistence on "emptiness" veered too much from the middle path toward nihilism, the Yogācāra argued that consciousness itself, rather than any external impulse, is somehow determinate of the objects we perceive, and vice-versa. This dualism of consciousness and its objects, particularly as analyzed by the Yogācāra master Vasubandhu,[28] is said to be mediated in some way by a common or nondual nature, out of which the mutual duality emerges of consciousness conditioned by objects and objects conditioned by consciousness. Liberation for the Yogācāra follows, it seems, upon the suspension of that duality through its resolution into some sort of a nondual consciousness. The Yogācāra were criticized in turn by Candrakīrti for reifying this nondual consciousness into an independently existing essence somehow generating our perceptions. Here we find a consistent application of the notion of "emptiness," ruling out any appeal to *any* sort of essence behind phenomena, whether understood objectively or subjectively, or even otherwise, as nonduality. For the Madhyamaka both the objects of consciousness and the consciousness of objects—as manifest in the *skandhas*—are entirely a matter of dependent origination, that is, of mutual cause and effect

conditioning, with no recourse to anything outside or beyond the
skandhas. Just as the Pyrrhonists insist upon distinguishing between
the evident and the nonevident to the point where any account of
things evident can be given only in terms of things evident, and not in
terms of anything nonevident, so the Madhyamaka too insist that dependent origination be wholly a matter of the skandhas, whose thoroughgoing "emptiness" precludes any appeal beyond themselves. Yet
the duality of consciousness observed by the Yogācāra is not banished,
but rather incorporated into what is evident. We cannot see beyond the
skandhas, as the Madhyamaka insist, but that does not preclude the
Yogācāra recognition of the subject of the skandhas, or consciousness;
it means rather than such a recognition must be an indeterminate one,
but not nothing.

—ɷɷɷ—

Let us look more closely at this curiously paradoxical experience of
the evidently nonevident. Anything that is evident, any appearance,
seems to be some kind of object of consciousness for both Pyrrhonists
and Buddhists. But consciousness famously is not itself among the objects that appear to it. For the Pyrrhonists, it remains indeterminate.
Consciousness for them seems to be equated with the soul [psuche],
which is also equated with activity, energy, or power. Although indeterminate, it is implied as the subject of the objects that appear. We—
each of us—seem to be a non-object or subject we call consciousness,
or the soul; "all perception is a property of the soul," Sextus tells us in
Against the Ethicists. He goes on to add that "the sense of intelligence
which apprehends the desirable is of the soul."[29] These and other similar comments, though made by Sextus more or less in passing, suggest
that he presumes the soul (psuche), though not an object, to be something of which we have some sort of knowledge. How can the soul be
evident and knowable, and not be a belief?

Sextus seems to reason as follows: It is neither a sensation nor a
thought. It may, however, in a negative sense, be something evidently
nonevident, which is to say, a no-thing which does not appear but
which is implied by anything and everything which does appear. Indeed, it seems we could not even speak of what is evident without implying some kind of experience of the nonevident. If any evident thing
is an appearance, it is an appearance, as we like to say, for us. The evident is what is in fact perceived, or can be perceived, leaving negative
or empty the notion of a perceiver. A nonevident perceiver—a self, a
soul, a consciousness—would be indeterminate, not an object or entity
in any way, though perhaps in some sense nonetheless undeniably

modified in some way, and so in some sense evident. This allows, Sextus suggests, a certain negative sense we have of ourselves as the non-objects or subjects we seem to be.

This subtle point bears explication. What is not evident about the self or soul is any claim to specify it as some sort of existing entity, similar to any number of other entities or abstract objects said to underlie appearances according to the dogmatists. Just as the combination of appearances we take to be an "apple" is only a combination of appearances, not the manifestation of some kind of independently existing essence or substance somehow underlying and sustaining those appearances, so the overall combination of appearances each of us experiences in totality, that is, all the sensations and thoughts of which we are comprised in our life-history as individuals, all this is still only a combination of appearances, and not any manifestation of some kind of independently existing essence or substance we might be tempted to call "soul" or "person" or "consciousness." In that sense, as with the Buddhists, there is no self. Sextus reminds us, when discussing the combination of sensible objects with intelligible ones in *Against the Logicians*, that the heterogeneity of these objects does not allow any inference to a common essence or substance of any sort: "For even if these faculties [the sensible and the intelligible] seem ever so much to be combined in the same substance and to be coextensive with each other and to range throughout the whole soul, none the less they are generically different from each other, this being one thing and that quite another."[30] We have no warrant, Sextus reminds us again and again, to leap from the combination of sensations and thoughts that seems to exhaust our inventory of the objects of which we are conscious to any characterization of consciousness, or soul, or self. We can learn nothing, it seems, about the soul from the objects of which it is conscious, or as the Pyrrhonists would say, which affect the soul.

Sextus seems to accept the soul, not as an independently existing entity of any sort, but as some kind of indeterminate subject that is nonetheless affected by its objects. These objects, or appearances, are explicitly said by Sextus to be modifications of the soul—involuntary experiences I must suffer—as we have seen.[31] In the *Outlines* he states plainly: "There are two things from which humans are said to be composed, soul and body."[32] And further: "For they [humans] are composed of soul and body; but neither bodies nor souls perhaps are apprehended."[33] Only appearances are apprehended, it seems, and from these we cannot get to bodies, or persons, or souls. Soul is not apprehended any more than body. But just as the appearances we have are undeniable because they are evident, at least to us, by that very fact it seems also undeniable that these appearances are ours, that it is we who have them because we are modified by them. "An appearance, then," Sextus tells us, "will actually be of the feeling of a sense—and this is different from an external existing object."[34] The underlying essences or substances of our experiences (e.g., any notion of an independently existing body or substance) seem to be fictions we cannot independently establish. But I can no more deny that I am having the appearance I am having as a feeling (*pathe*) than I can deny the appearance itself, and this is because the appearance is a modification of my self. To suspend judgment about the self or soul is not to say that some kind of modification does not occur to us with any appearance. It is only to say that we cannot characterize the self that is so modified in any way, except negatively, as that non-object which is evidently nonevident to us as the subject of our appearances.

Sextus carefully avoids any attempt to specify what the evident might be, not wishing to fall into dogmatic assertion. He is content most of the time with pointing to the evident as we encounter it here and there, with examples, with reminding us that what is evident is primarily our direct or present or unmediated and involuntary experience of sensations and thoughts. But we also seem to experience ourselves as perceiving subjects, as he acknowledges, which suggests a more complex sense of what is evident. Fortunately, there is one passage, in *Against the Logicians*, where Sextus goes further and offers the following interesting fourfold observations of the evident and the nonevident: "there are four distinct classes of objects [*pragmata*, or 'facts']—one being that of things manifest, the second of things absolutely nonevident, the third of things naturally nonevident, the fourth of things temporarily so."[35] Let us follow Sextus closely here. Things manifest, that is, evident, are our direct sensations and thoughts as we have them. Things temporarily nonevident are those we normally expect will or can be made evident again, having once been evident. Sextus gives the example of the city of Athens as temporarily nonevident to his readers or auditors, suggesting that he was speaking or writing somewhere far removed from Athens; of course, Athens would become evident to someone who actually journeyed to the city. Then there are things absolutely nonevident, which turn out to be "things whose nature is never to be presented to human apprehension, as is the fact that the stars are even in number or odd, and that the grains of sand in Libya are of a certain definite number."[36] And finally, the fourth sort of object or fact we can distinguish is that of things naturally nonevident, namely, those which are "everlastingly hidden away and are not capable of presenting themselves clearly to our perception, such as the intelligible pores and the existence . . . of an infinite Void outside the universe."[37] He adds to this last: "The soul, for instance, is one of the things naturally nonevident; for such is its nature that it never presents itself to our clear perception."[38] The absolute and naturally nonevident seem to be evident in an important sense, that is, to be evidently nonevident.

Things naturally nonevident are just as unavailable (unmanifest) as those absolutely nonevident, but in the former case we lack even the sort of potential context for things that we find for things absolutely nonevident. Although stars and grains of sand are manifest objects of consciousness, they cannot all simultaneously be manifest in such a way as would allow us to count them, which is what we would need to do to make evident whether they are odd or even, or of a certain specific number. What makes objects absolutely nonevident is that we can see both what we need to do to make the required determination, and also thereby that we cannot do it. Dogmatists presumably can see this as well as sceptics, Sextus seems to presume, so there is no controversy over absolutely nonevident things, no beliefs about them that are likely to be propounded, let alone taken seriously. The problem arises rather with the remaining group, with naturally nonevident things. Here we cannot see what we need to do to make the required determination, and so neither can we see that we cannot do it. Into this breach rush the dogmatists, offering one belief after another for what it is that the naturally nonevident—the Void, God, the Soul, the Body, and so on—might be. The naturally or evidently nonevident is for us an absence conditioned by the possible presence of an object. It is negatively evident, that is, evident only as a lack, perhaps, metaphorically, in the way that a photographic negative is evidence of the lack of the positive photographic print. Space, for instance, makes no sense unless there are objects to appear and disappear in space. Once an object appears, so does space; the object establishes a boundary between itself, what is inside it, and what is not-itself, what is outside it, so that the defined something which is the object finds itself mutually conditioned by the undefined nothing which is not the object. Evident things, then—those objects which appear—necessarily imply or make evident to us as well what is nonevident, though only as an absence, like a trace, a footprint in the sand.

In the Madhyamaka texts we similarly find a place for what is evidently nonevident, which is called the "emptiness" (śūnyatā) of things, that is, the nothingness which is implied by the lack of substance of phenomena, but which is nonetheless a nothingness that is a kind of something insofar as it is an absence created and conditioned by the presence which phenomenal things enjoy. Consciousness is included as one of the *skandhas*, as a dependent aspect of phenomenal experience, even though it does not have the kind of determinate presence we find in the objects of our experience, that is, in our sensations and thoughts. It is conspicuously not an object. Consciousness itself famously does not appear as an item among the objects of consciousness, as Hume pointed out. The Madhyamaka notion of "emptiness" then can therefore be understood, I suggest, as an instance—perhaps the most fundamental—of what the Pyrrhonists call the naturally or evidently nonevident. Since something is conditioned by nothing, and nothing by something, no thing can be completely or wholly something, any more than nothing can be completely or wholly nothing. And here, perhaps, we see a hint of the nonduality of the Yogācāra. The Yogācāra writer Maitreya, in his *Analysis of the Middle and Extremes* [*Madhyānta-vibhāga*], tells us explicitly that emptiness is "the non-being of subject and object and the being of that nonbeing."[39] Furthermore, a whole tradition of Buddhism, the Pudgalavādans, recognized what they called the reality of the indeterminate self.[40] So we see, perhaps, that the liberation from suffering promoted by both Buddhists and Pyrrhonists depends crucially on distinguishing between consciousness and the objects of consciousness, between what is evident and what is evidently nonevident. In Buddhist language, neither "eternalism" nor "annihiliationism" makes sense. The Buddhist middle path is also, it seems, the path of the Pyrrhonist. The "emptiness" of the evidently nonevident is only the "emptiness" of its nonobjectivity, its indeterminacy. Like antimatter, it is a complementary aspect of experience, giving us the only self we can distinguish, obscure and dependent as it may be to us who are distracted by objects, but nonetheless with a claim to some kind of being of its own.

—◈◈◈—

But how is it is possible in the first place for a positive or negative dogmatist (an "eternalist" or an "annihiliationist") to make claims about what is nonevident, and so confuse the evident with the nonevident? Both Pyrrhonists and Buddhists agree that this can occur only insofar as the dogmatist is able to propound a sign—a token, a mark, a word, a view, a story, a theory, etc.—which then can be claimed to represent some nonevident reality, and which thereby supports belief, that is, renders plausible, at least minimally, the notion that it represents something. Without signs, it appears, we cannot form beliefs about things nonevident. We don't need signs for things manifest, Sextus observes, precisely because they are manifest, and so do not stand in need of recollection or recall. Nor do we need signs for what is absolutely nonevident, it being evident to all that such things cannot be signified. We need signs, he says, only for absent things which have been and could be manifest, but are not now so—the temporarily nonevident. But the dogmatists think we also need signs for the naturally or evidently nonevident, for emptiness.

In the *Outlines*, Sextus discusses these two kinds of signs, calling them the recollective and the indicative. (*In Against the Logicians*, he calls these same recollective signs "commemorative."[41]) "They [all philosophers, including the Pyrrhonists] call a sign recollective," he says, "if, having been observed evidently together with the thing it signifies, at the same time as it makes an impression on us—and while the other thing remains unclear—it leads us to recall the thing which has been observed together with it and is not now making an evident impression on us (as in the case of smoke and fire)."[42] And by contrast: "A sign is indicative, they [the dogmatists, but not the Pyrrhonists] say, if it signifies that of which it is a sign not by having been observed evidently together with the thing it signifies but from its proper nature and constitution (as bodily movements are signs of the soul)."[43] He makes it plain that "we [the Pyrrhonists] argue not against all signs but only against indicative signs, which seem to be a fiction of the Dogmatists."[44]

We can have meaningful signs, according to Sextus, only for things that are temporarily nonevident. All that is necessary for a sign to signify something temporarily nonevident is that the sign and the thing signified have been or can be "observed evidently together." This happens naturally in the consistent association of the normal appearances we experience: the bundles of thoughts and sensations which constitute the perceptual world, the more or less repetitive cycles of objects and events which constitute the round of life. It also happens with cultural conventions. A child is taught the alphabet when he or she learns to associate together certain otherwise arbitrary visual marks with certain otherwise arbitrary audible sounds, and only after this association is established can he or she take these visual and audible "letters" as signs of one another. Such an association of otherwise uncorrelated appearances—a convention—is what allows us to take one of them as a reliable token or sign for the other in its absence, as we do when we take smoke as a sign of a fire we cannot see, or a scar as a sign of a wound we have not seen inflicted, or a picture or map of Athens as a sign of the city we have not yet visited, or the visual letters CAT for the sound we pronounce "*kat*," and so on. In all these cases, when one evident thing is used as a sign for another, temporarily nonevident one, it is only because the two things have been, or can be made to be, mutually or simultaneously evident together. (We can see arbitrary convention of such association in cultural constructs such as the alphabet because we create them, but the world into which we are born seems just as arbitrarily associated together, except that we did not create it.) Again, this is the only kind of sign we need, Sextus tells us in *Against the Logicians*, and the only kind that really functions as a sign:

> As it is, then, seeing that we affirm the commemorative [e.g., recollective] sign which ordinary folk employ, but abolish the sign falsely imagined by the Dogmatists, one should rather say that not only do we not attack ordinary life but we even act as its advocates, inasmuch as we refute by means of natural science the Dogmatists who have risen up against the common judgment and declared that they discern by means of signs things naturally non-evident.[45]

When the dogmatists postulate that their indicative signs should be taken to represent nonevident things of one sort or another, they require belief since they cannot provide, that is, actually make evident, the nonevident things in question, but only a proposed token for them. They propose a signifier, say the word "soul," but can produce no evident corresponding signified, no actual soul. The signifier in this case is an empty placeholder, but one for which we can arbitrarily imagine or abstract some kind of content which we cannot substantiate. A dogmatist might say that the word "soul" represents the self-contained life-force found in a living thing, or, alternatively, an incorporeal entity which survives the death of the body, and so on. Since any number of such contents can be projected into the empty space created by an indicative sign, the dogmatists who make these claims end up with conflicting and often contradictory accounts of what they believe to be signified by such signs. Given their equivalent plausibility, or lack thereof, it is only prudent, says the Pyrrhonian sceptic, to suspend judgment about such beliefs. The only way the word "soul" could be a sign of something we call the soul is if the latter turned out to be a manifest or evident fact, a differentiated, determinate entity of some sort present to consciousness, something we could observe directly, an appearance.

Even if we understand the soul as evidently nonevident, as present to consciousness but indeterminate, our sign for it necessarily remains empty, can literally have no content, no determinative, distinguishing character. Nor can we even say it signifies nothing, since the evidently nonevident seems to be something, though nothing determinate. A sign for the evidently nonevident has no efficacy, therefore, and can only mislead by suggesting some kind of determinate content. A sign for the evidently nonevident is a sign for a suspended judgment; indeed, it is a sign which itself should be suspended. Terms for the evidently nonevident, such as "soul" or "emptiness" are inherently self-defeating if we think they can be of any use at all. Sextus no doubt would agree with Nāgārjuna, who advises us that "'Empty' should not be asserted. 'Nonempty' should not be asserted. Neither both nor either should be asserted."[46] At the end of his *Tractatus*, in an oft-cited passage, Wittgenstein makes the same point as follows: "My propositions serve as elucidations in the following say: anyone who understands me eventually recognizes them as nonsensical, when he has used them—as steps—to climb up beyond them. (He must, so to speak, throw away the ladder after he has climbed up it.) He must transcend these propositions, and then he will see the world aright. What we cannot speak about we must pass over in silence."[47]

Signs are relative to one another, a Pyrrhonist point it is hard to exaggerate. We have a sign and thing signified, just as we have left and right, whole and part, cause and effect, etc. But there is no such thing as a sign in itself, or a sign without a thing signified; there is only the use of one evident thing to signify another temporarily nonevident thing. Signification as such is not evident because it is a relation, and relations themselves are nonevident—a point, as we shall see further in the next chapter, made by Wittgenstein in his well-known contrast between what can be said and what can be shown. Just as we can be confident that our recollective signs signify certain appearances—as smoke signifies fire and the scar a wound—there is no appearance of signification as such, that is, there is no specific appearance of which we can say *it* is signification itself, the way we can say that this specific visual appearance is a tree, that audible appearance is laughter, and so on. "Sign" and "signification" have no independent existence; they are like so many other nonevident beliefs proposed by dogmatists, including criteria, wholes and parts, proof, God, motion, truth, Man, causation, and so on. Just as we cannot find causation itself as a discrete item anywhere in the chain of causes and effects as if it were a specific one of the many links in the chain rather than what it is, namely, the relative nature of how all those links stand to one another (say straight, curved, taut, loose, direct, delayed, etc.), just so we cannot find the sign itself as one appearance among the others signified. And similarly, it seems, for every dogmatic belief that comes along. Perhaps most fundamental of all the Pyrrhonist arguments is the relativity of signs, for signs include all other relations, which can be expressed only as signs, that is, only through some sort of notation or symbolism or language. Animals, for instance, mostly lacking signs, presumably mostly lack beliefs.

And indeed, the origin of the various Pyrrhonian modes—those groups of stock arguments, or talking points—comes out of the relational character of dogmatic beliefs expressed through signs, that is, through language and other notations, including mathematics and geometry. In the *Outlines*, Sextus gives a detailed account of the famous ten modes, and also discusses the five modes of Aggripa, and the eight modes of Aenesidemus. The modes are presented rather abruptly and discontinuously, with little indication of where they come from, and scholars have treated them largely as a set of more or less arbitrary or stock arguments, some more effective, in their opinion, and others less so. Sextus discusses the modes only in his *Outlines*. We are told, as we have seen, that they consist in "the opposition of things. We oppose what appears to what appears, or what is thought of to what is thought of, or crosswise."[48] Once the relevant oppositions are presented, debate is neutralized, and the observer is justified in suspending judgment, after which tranquility is said to supervene.

The style of the modes and their psychological effect in frustrating claims about the nonevident and liberating the disputants is well illustrated in a story retold by Sextus about a rhetorician named Corax:

A young man seized with a desire for rhetoric went to him [Corax] and promised that he would pay him the fee he would charge, if he should win his first case. And when the compact was made, and the youth was now displaying sufficient skill, Corax demanded his fee, but the other said "No." Both then repaired to the court and had the cased tried; and then, it is said, Corax first used an argument of this kind,—that whether he won the case or lost it he ought to receive the fee; if he won, because he had won, and if he lost, in accordance with the terms of the compact; for his opponent had agreed to pay him the fee if he won his first case, so that if he did win it he was thereby bound to discharge the debt. And after the judges had applauded him for speaking justly the young man in turn began his speech and used the same argument, altering nothing: "Whether I win," he says, "or whether I am beaten, I am not bound to pay Corax the fee; if I win, because I have won, and if I lose, in accordance with the terms of the compact; for I promised to pay the fee if I should win my first case, but if I should lose I shall not pay." The judges then, thrown into a state of suspense and perplexity, owing to the equipollence of the theoretical arguments, drove them both out of the court.[49]

The Pyrrhonists recognized various modes of argumentation, though no list seems to have been inclusive or determinative. The ten modes are the best known. They comprise a series of contrasts or differences: 1) among animals, 2) among humans, 3) among sense organs, 4) among circumstances, 5) among spatial relations, 6) among admixtures, 7) among quantities, 8) among relative things, 9) among encounters, and 10) among our "persuasions and customs and laws and belief in myths and dogmatic suppositions."[50] In his discussion of the ten modes, Sextus gives us a very interesting ranking of the modes, with the ten modes ultimately collapsed into one super-mode, as it were:

> Superordinate to these [ten] are three modes: that deriving from the subject judging; that deriving from the object judged; that combined from both. For under the mode deriving from the subject judging are ranged the first four, for what judges is either an animal or a human or a sense, and is in some circumstance. The seventh and tenth are referred to the mode deriving from the object judged. The fifth, sixth, eighth, and ninth are referred to the mode combined from both. These three are in turn referred to the relativity mode. So we have as most generic relativity, as specific the three, as subordinate the ten.[51]

Relativity—we might also say with the Buddhists "dependent origination"—is here presented as the ultimate super-mode. It is the mode of which the others are but parts, and no doubt the modes of Aggripa and Aenesidemus could be folded into this ultimate mode as well. If we consider what we have been saying about the evident and nonevident in this chapter, and the nature of signs in the context of what is evident and nonevident, we can see that the modes are about whether a purported sign has in fact corresponding to it an evident or manifest signified. When Sextus tells us that "we oppose what appears to what appears, or what is thought of to what is thought of, or crosswise," he is telling us that the Pyrrhonist always looks for sensations and/or thoughts, for what is evident, corresponding to any assertion which is made about how things are. An assertion is a complex purported sign, after all. If I say "the human soul is immortal," the Pyrrhonist is first of all aware that this is an asserted but not necessarily an actual sign, a proposition which is itself an appearance (something which is spoken or written), and which is purported by some, at least, to represent something temporarily nonevident, which somehow could be made evident. The question is: Can something evident be produced to cash in that claim? If it cannot, then the sign is empty or null, a fiction, which can be filled with contradictory notions. If it can be produced, then we are dealing not with something naturally nonevident, but with something temporarily nonevident, with which Pyrrhonists have no quarrel.

The possibility of contradiction arises because the failure to produce the temporarily nonevident opens the possibility that it may variously be characterized. The signifier, the proposition, may be put one way, or perhaps another: "The cat is not on the mat." "The cat on the mat is black." "The cat on the mat is white." And so on. When varying and conflicting signifiers corresponding to a single signified arise, the search for the supposedly temporarily nonevident is intensified. Just where is that cat? Just what color is it? We want to resolve the uncertainty. If the uncertainty is not resolved, if the variations and contradictions multiply, then, when the claims are serious, anxiety develops, often with increasingly untoward consequences. But by opposing these varieties and contradictions, by showing that the signifier can variously and inconsistently be projected, the absence of the signified is demonstrated, though negatively only (we see that it is not and perhaps cannot be manifest), and only with regard to the various claims advanced. Judgment can then be suspended, and tranquility can, at least on that point, supervene.

Signification, then, can both elucidate and anticipate the evident and also enable the confusion of the evident with the nonevident. Science is about elucidating and anticipating what is evident, including what can be made evident through signs; it is the explicit development of our system of recollective signs to represent correlations among appearances not otherwise representable to us. To show that something believed to be evident cannot (at least yet) be made evident, that it appears in fact to be nonevident, is to show that is it not science. Of course most people, perhaps all of us, even the most knowledgeable and experienced, even those recognized and honored as scientists, confuse to varying degrees the evident and the nonevident; it is largely the human condition to do so, of course, a dilemma for which Pyrrhonism, like Buddhism, offers itself as a therapeutic remedy. Somewhat briefly in the *Outlines* and at greater length in *Against the Physicists*, Sextus considers the dogmatic presumptions of the scientists of his day— including Anaxagoras, Empedocles, Aristotle, Democritus, Pythagoreans, Epicureans, and Stoics, among many others—and finds a series of dogmatic beliefs in their works, including beliefs in God, intelligent design, causality, geometrical and numerical abstractions, forms and ideas, wholes and parts, bodies, space and time, motion, change, among many others.

This Pyrrhonian deconstruction of the beliefs of the scientists of antiquity by separating, as much as possible, the evident from the nonevident, is paralleled by similar deconstructions of the dogmatic beliefs of logicians and ethicists. All of these groups are treated succinctly if briefly in the *Outlines*, and in greater detail in *Against the Physicists*, and *Against the Ethicists*. In his other surviving work, *Against the Professors*, Sextus considers the dogmatic beliefs of grammarians and writers, rhetoricians, geometers, mathematicians, astrologers, and musicians, most of whom are not treated in the *Outlines*. All these areas of human endeavor, from logic to science to rhetoric to music, depend upon signs to articulate their claims; they are all notational systems of one sort or another; they all claim to speak about their subject matters (Sextus' focus in music, for instance, is not on performance, or music as such, but on what is said and believed about music). Whether we speak in terms of the sciences or the arts, or even when we practice some of them, such as rhetoric, or even in ordinary speech, we are speaking about something, it is presumed, hopefully something temporally nonevident, and therefore employing signs of some sort, which leads naturally into the crucial Pyrrhonist queries about whether the signified is indeed about something temporally nonevident, or about something naturally nonevident.

The depth and scope of our dogmatic beliefs in nonevident things—our belief that the signs we posit for such things have a content—according to Pyrrhonists (and Buddhists) is hard to exaggerate. Some beliefs are universally accepted. Most everyone once took the world to be flat. Most people today presume an independently existing external material reality. Newtonian absolute space and time were accepted by practically the entire scientific and cultural community in the West for hundreds of years. Fundamentalists accept a literal reading of the Bible, Talmud, or Koran. Some kind of ultimate god or being has commanded belief very widely for thousands of years in many cultures. Secular ideologues ask us to believe in "the free market" or "the American way of life" or secular humanism. And so on with many other beliefs—almost an endless number—we could cite. Pyrrhonists themselves are willing to accept, or at least respect, the customs and mores of the society in which they find themselves. Many of these—such as language or a monetary system or units of measure, etc.—are arbitrary but useful systems for the most part conducive to the satisfaction of needs, and for the securing of what is temporally nonevident. Others indeed reflect beliefs, such as religious or patriotic rituals, but the Pyrrhonists can accept these pragmatically or not, depending on circumstances. As always, the challenge is to examine claims that are made to see if they are factual matters or matters of belief. Even the most deeply and widely held beliefs are subject to challenge by contradiction, at which point they become objectified, attacked and defended, problematic, and distressing, a source of suffering, but also open to relief by suspension of judgment.

Signification is as central to Buddhist attachment as it is to Pyrrhonist belief. Sue Hamilton, a scholar of early Buddhism, writes that "according to the early texts, all worldly experience is structured accordingly to the characteristics of name and form [nāma-rūpa]."[52] More expansively, she tells us "that in early Buddhism, as in the pre-Buddhist understanding of name-and-form, the entirety of cyclical experience—the world of subjectivity and objectivity—is organized according to, and understood by means of, a name-and-form structure . . . one might say that what the world of subjectivity and objectivity is characterized by is named form(s)."[53] "So name-and-form," she says, "is the structure that underpins the manifold world of experience."[54] Name-and-form, or nāma-rūpa, is noted in the earliest texts, she reminds us—going back to the Buddha's announcement of the Four Noble Truths in his first sermon.[55] She argues that it a crucial, perhaps the crucial, move in the process of dependent origination, which includes all experience as we know it. Without the ability to name, that is to signify, we would not be able to take things signified as definitive objects persisting even in their absence.

Let me elaborate on her point. The object may not be present—as in the Pyrrhonian notion of things temporarily nonevident—but the name, which is present more or less at will, encourages the illusion of the object's accompanying presence, which illusion easily slides into the assertion of some kind of ongoing presence, or independent existence, of the object. Naming allows us to purport to signify various nonevident things, as we have seen, including what the Pyrrhonists classify as naturally or evidently nonevident, as well as those absolutely nonevident. The Buddhist texts tend to assert or simply list the components of experience, the *skandhas* and dependent origination, in formulaic ways for the most part, with relatively little discussion of just how dependent origination and the *skandhas* work as a dynamic process. The burden of Hamilton's work is to reconstruct that process. The Buddha's breakthrough to enlightenment, to seeing the causes and remedy for human suffering, did not negate the human world in which the Buddha, after all, continued to live and thrive and teach for the next forty-five years. Presumably for him, as for the Pyrrhonists, the kind of signification we use for things temporarily nonevident is natural and valid, and not itself a cause of suffering; it itself ought not to generate the *saṃsāric* quality of experience we seek to relieve. So insofar as signification is crucial to attachment and thereby suffering, it must be the other kind of signification that is responsible, the signification of natural or evidently nonevident things, of which the self or soul is among the most conspicuous. These are the significations that are matters of belief, that is, of assertion and will-ful projection, of determinations, attributions, and characterizations of one sort or another about things persistently and consistently non-evident, treated as if they were or somehow could be made so.

Signification of naturally or evidently nonevident things seems to be the mechanism, for Buddhists and Pyrrhonists alike, by which be-liefs are produced; these beliefs distract us from sensory and thought experience and impose various unsubstantiated views which distort our judgments and reactions to that experience. Ignorance with regard to actual objects of our beliefs (to our attachments) is what allows us to take them as if they were independently existing entities, even if not evident to us. Buddhist practice, including meditative practice, is aimed at revealing our beliefs as beliefs, not as facts, and so liberating us from them. Experience is not thereby extinguished, but its dis-ease, that which makes it *dukkha*, is relieved. A great deal of Buddhist lit-erature, particularly in older English translations, leaves the misim-pression that liberation from *saṃsāra* is somehow equivalent to the extinction of sensory and thought experience; our Pyrrhonist texts, by contrast, leave no doubt that *ataraxia*, as important a relief to suffer-ing as it is, frees no one from the normal pains of physical existence. Buddhism makes better sense, it would seem, if we understand that the liberation it offers is similarly confined to the relief experienced following our suspension of judgment over contentious beliefs. In his long life after enlightenment, the Buddha was no more exempt from aches and pains than anyone else. In both traditions the ability to bear such pains seems greatly enhanced by liberation from beliefs, perhaps to the point where physical pain, though not eliminated, is reduced for the subject to a kind of sensation much more easily, if not effortlessly, borne.

—⟐—

If my attempts in this chapter to elucidate the Pyrrhonian and Bud-dhist distinction between the evident and nonevident have any merit, we might wonder what kind of way of life anyone seeking to follow these nondogmatic soteriological practices could lead, given this land-scape, as it were, of appearances and consciousness and its limits. As we have earlier noted, Sextus near the beginning of the *Outlines* gives an oft-cited four-point program of how Pyrrhonists "live in accordance with everyday observances, without holding opinions," which in-cludes "guidance by nature, necessitation of feelings, handing down of laws and customs, and teaching of kinds of expertise." He then offers a brief but important elucidation: "By nature's guidance we are naturally capable of perceiving and thinking. By the necessitation of feelings, hunger conducts us to food and thirst to drink. By the handing down of customs and laws, we accept, from an everyday point of view, that piety is good and impiety bad. And by teaching of kinds of expertise we are not inactive in those which we accept."[56] It is worth reviewing each of these points in light of what we have found to be evident and nonevident in Pyrrhonism, as represented by Sextus. I will conclude by comparing briefly the Buddhist way of life with the Pyrrhonist.

The first point, that through which "we are naturally capable of perceiving and thinking," is simply the recognition of our sensations and thoughts, of our direct, immediate, involuntary objects of experience, our appearances, just as they are present to us. Pyrrhonists, as we have seen, find no reason to doubt these appearances. They say they are unavoidably evident to us. Explicating the point that "we are naturally capable of perceiving and thinking" what is evident (as opposed to the nonevident) has been a principal burden of this chapter. The second point recognizes that these same objects—sensations and thoughts—are "feelings," or various modifications of our consciousness, which are variously compelling to us. They belong to us; they are ours; they are inalienable. They are the objects of which we are the subjects. In our experience, at any rate, there seem to be no objects without subjects (no independently existing objects), and no subjects without objects (without appearances).

To be (an object, an appearance) is to be perceived (by a subject, a perceiver who is not perceived). We, the subjects, necessarily and involuntarily react to our objects, to our sensations and thoughts; we are modified by them. Although that reaction can be one of neutrality, it is more likely to be some kind of more or less decentering compulsion: pleasure or pain, fear or elation, etc. Thus our reaction to the natural world is inseparable from our perceiving and thinking it. We can and sometimes should resist these compulsions, it is true, but it is usually foolish to ignore them, as it would be foolish to ignore thirst or hunger or sex. We must choose to allow in some ways at least some of our compulsions if we are to survive. The third point concerns the world of human convention, which the Pyrrhonist accepts, though only "from an everyday point of view." These social conventions, manifest as appearances and behaviors, include all the artificial structures of human intercourse, from language to kinship to society and law and custom. These too can and no doubt sometimes should be resisted, but someone who refuses to obey the laws of a country, who chooses not to speak its language, or use its money, or calculate with its number system, etc., would for the most part be acting as foolishly as some one who tried to ignore his hunger in hopes that it would go away. A toleration of a variety of human conventions suggests a "when in Rome do as the Romans do" attitude.

Are there any limits to what a Pyrrhonist might tolerate? It might appear not, yet a Pyrrhonist cannot help but adhere to what is evident, and to eschew nonevident beliefs. This is the only guide they offer. In the face of violence and pain and cruelty, for instance, as witnessed in the arenas of the ancient Romans, the Pyrrhonist, with beliefs about what he or she is witnessing suspended, presumably would be free to react more fully and appropriately to the involuntary sensory aspects of the spectacle. There would be no rationalizing away the experience. For most people, one hopes, in the absence of rationalizing, soothing, or distracting dogmatic beliefs about what is going on, there would be revulsion and disgust. Without holding to any belief about the spectacle (gladiator shows had their origin and justification in the funerary rites of noble families), the repulsiveness of the spectacle would be able to speak for itself. Of course a sadist, say, would be attracted rather than repelled by the spectacle, but sadists are the exception not the norm, not a good measure of human value. We don't judge the taste of an apple by the rotten parts. Pyrrhonists would ask to what degree a condition such as sadism might be a function of belief. A population of Pyrrhonists, we might expect, not being distracted by beliefs that might justify or encourage the spectacle, would generally turn away, and perhaps out of compassion seek to end such cruel practices.

What would a Pyrrhonist do, more broadly, in the face of a modern totalitarian regime such as the Soviet Union or Nazi Germany? Or in the face of human injustice, as in conditions of slavery, segregation, exploitation, corruption, or preemptive war? The conventional response has been that the Pyrrhonist would have to "go along" insofar as he or she simply followed the conventions of society. But here too we should recall that the Pyrrhonist makes a point of not acting out of beliefs informing such behavior. Lacking a belief, say, in the "dictatorship of the proletariat" or the "master race" or the "free market," the Pyrrhonist, suspending all such notions, would use none of them as a criterion of action. Again, he or she would act out of direct experience, taking situations at face value. One would expect the Pyrrhonist to turn away from acts of injustice motivated by various beliefs, and even resist them. In *Against the Ethicists*, Sextus tells us that "one must scorn those who fancy that he [the Pyrrhonist] is confined to a state of inactivity or of inconsistency."[57] We should "scorn" such critics since the Pyrrhonist, Sextus points out, "does not conduct his life according to philosophical theory . . . but as regards the non-philosophical regulation of life he is capable of desiring some things and avoiding others."[58] So when confronted for instance with the demands of a tyrant to do something unspeakable or face the consequences, he will not avoid action but "perchance choose the one course and avoid the other owing to the preconception due to his ancestral laws and customs."[59]

This has sounded disappointing to modern critics,[60] but it is no more than the claim that the Pyrrhonist will act in accordance with his or her experience of appearances, including the context of those appearances, and not in accordance with his or her beliefs about those appearances. No rule of behavior such as a dogmatist might presume is expected here. The tyrant presents only bad choices; any beliefs we hold about them, it seems, only cancel out one another. The Pyrrhonist can evaluate the choices only in relation to other appearances with which they can be compared, and these will differ from person to person; we might summarize them as the force of one's culture and character, the historical weight of "ancestral laws and customs." There might be good reasons, Sextus suggests, to do the tyrant's bidding, however horrible, perhaps to save loved ones; equally there may be reasons to resist the tyrant's will, if it seems that doing it would lead to consequences even more terrible. The Pyrrhonist acts in light of his or her particular history; to suspend beliefs about that history is to remove superfluous and distracting motives for acting one way or another. Sextus is arguing that there is nothing passive or paralyzing about the Pyrrhonist way of life, as indeed there was nothing passive about Pyrrho's coming to the vigorous defense of his sister Philista when she was criticized.[61] The Pyrrhonist leads a fully active life, but it is informed by spontaneous reaction to experience, not by beliefs about that experience.

The fourth and final point with regard to how the Pyrrhonist should live, concerning the teaching of various kinds of "expertise," is perfectly consistent with the Pyrrhonists' scientific outlook. The uncovering of hitherto unknown correlations between things that can be made evident is a skill or science, a way to deepen our knowledge of experience. Sextus' philosophy of science deserves to be further explored. It insists upon evident correlations among appearances, without trying to define appearances, as the basis of any kind of valid scientific assertion. The important of science is not generally highlighted by Sextus, yet he was an empirically oriented physician, and an empirical, scientific outlook lies at the heart of the Pyrrhonist critique of dogmatism in its many forms, including what we would now call "scientism." "[N]ot only do we not attack ordinary life," Sextus tells us in *Against the Logicians*, "but we even act as its advocates, inasmuch as we refute by means of natural science the Dogmatists who have risen up against the common judgment and declared that they discern by means of signs things naturally nonevident."[62]

―――⟐⟐⟐―――

What kind of way of life can we discover in all this? It is above all a life in which beliefs are suspended rather than affirmed or denied, a life without belief, a free life, Pyrrhonists would say. The Pyrrhonist suspends judgment (*epochē*) with regard to beliefs, after which tranquility (*ataraxia*) is said to supervene. Absent the need to choose between beliefs (pro or con) about the nonevident, one is liberated from the consequences of such choices. Instead of living in the fog of belief, in the contentious world of the asserted nonevident, the Pyrrhonist lives in the evident world, taking his or her cue from what does or can appear. This life is no panacea; pains still accompany pleasures, and death remains the end of life, ever mysterious. What remains is the involuntary world of appearances; from the perspective of our bodies, we ride the flow of appearances, of the evident. The Pyrrhonist insistence on the involuntary nature of appearances can be understood to parallel the Buddhist insistence on life as suffering. The point is not that suffering is pain (for it can be pleasure as well); rather it is that suffering is involuntary experience. To suffer is to bear something, to submit to it. Once we suffer an appearance, our only choice, it seems, is to affirm it or tolerate it; we cannot wholly ignore it. We might profess to deny it, but we cannot not have the appearance. We affirm it by having a belief about it (that such-and-such is "the truth," or "divine," or "destiny," etc., or perhaps, in a negative affirmation, we believe that we can deny such-and-such altogether, decree it to be nothing). By contrast to this culture of belief, Pyrrhonists tolerate appearances (accept them without adhering to them) by eschewing any beliefs we might have about them, while acknowledging that they force themselves involuntarily upon us. To be released from beliefs, to achieve tranquility, is to suspend judgment about whether any appearance in particular is good or bad for us.

Buddhism too, most explicitly in the Mahāyāna and especially the Madhyamaka, is a call to a life without belief. By insisting on the dependent origination of all evident things, and thereby their emptiness, including what is evidently nonevident such as the self, Buddhism follows the Pyrrhonist acceptance of "guidance by nature." The interdependency of experience includes its transience, its constant exposure to change and revision; this parallels the Pyrrhonist claim that all things are relative to one another. There is vastly more Buddhist literature than Pyrrhonist, and much of it strikes a decidedly ascetic tone, in spite of the neutrality of the "middle path" in comparison to the dogmatic extremes of anniliationists and eternalists. But some Buddhist traditions, particularly in the Mahāyāna, preserve a more generous attitude towards experience, one that may go back to the Buddha himself. In *The Holy Teaching of Vimalakīrti*, for instance, we encounter in the figure of Vimalakirti a robust character, not a monk but a householder, someone immersed in the ordinary world, seemingly free of physical self-denial, yet fully enlightened.[63]

What the Pyrrhonists call "necessitation of feelings" can be correlated with what is left of the world of evident experience for Buddhists once all attachments have been overcome. The sage who has reached *nirvāṇa* continues to live in the real world, after all, as the karmic cycle from which he or she has been freed continues to play out, albeit without further input from him or her. The enlightened person has no need of volition; it is enough now to be a witness. Experience without belief, or the *skandhas* without attachments, is just the world as it comes in dependent origination. As far as "customs and laws" are concerned, Buddhists like Pyrrhonists are seemingly content to acknowledge the civility of normal social convention. But here too there can be no justification for endorsing "customs and laws" rooted in attachment and belief. The Dalai Lama has been turned into a political activist by his exile from Tibet; he cannot accept the legitimacy of Chinese rule, it would seem, insofar as its belief-based system distorts the reality of life not only for Tibetans but for Chinese as well. And as for the "teaching of kinds of expertise" by the Pyrrhonists, the Buddhists too teach skillful practices, not least being meditation, aimed as relieving beliefs and the suffering that follows from them. The ending of belief for the Pyrrhonists is equivalent, I suggest, to the ending of attachment for the Buddhists.

Finally, for both Pyrrhonists and Buddhists, liberation from beliefs or attachments into *ataraxia* or *nirvāṇa* brings about a suspension of willful activity. In both traditions, willful activity is fundamentally an intentional distortion of experience, a forcing of some kind of distorting interpretation or theory or myth onto experience, a willful assertion that some belief about experience must trump experience itself. Once such views are suspended, there is no need to distort experience, leaving us free to experience the natural flow of thoughts and sensations. Instead one is able to react spontaneously and, it is implied, appropriately, to the stimulus offered by sensations and thoughts understood in terms of dependent origination. What we understand as the will in either tradition does not, it seems, have any function except a distorting one. In the end the will is unnecessary. We cannot assert the nonevident positively or negatively, it seems, but we can still choose not to assert, to suspend judgment. If we conflate belief with attachment, we can see that Buddhism, particularly in its Madhyamaka version, can be understood as a technique for eliminating our willful affirmation of beliefs concerning nonevident things. As Sue Hamilton puts it: "the senses are referred to metaphorically as 'doors' (dvara). . . . And these 'doors,' by which all experience is mediated, need to be 'guarded.' . . . 'guarding' refers to the way one interprets and responds to one's experience. The aim is to understand the process as it is and not to become involved in affective, and therefore binding, responses to anything that is a part of one's experience: to as it were disengage the affective response from the cognitive operation."[64] Both traditions, in returning us to what is evident, including the evidently nonevident, offer a liberation not only from out beliefs, but from the narcissistic will which empowers them.

## NOTES

1. Immanuel Kant, *Critique of Pure Reason*, trans. Norman Kemp Smith (New York: St. Martin's Press, 1965), 93.
2. For Aristotle's view that any thing is a substance composed of a synthesis of form and matter, see his *Metaphysics*, Book Zeta.
3. On the rediscovery of Pyrrhonism in modern times and the uses to which it has been put, cf. Richard Popkin, *The History of Scepticism From Savonarola to Bayle*, rev. ed. (Oxford: Oxford University Press, 2003); I discuss Popkin's work in the next chapter.
4. Sextus Empiricus, *Outlines of Scepticism* (I, xi), 9.
5. Ibid. (I, x), 8.
6. Sextus Empiricus, *Against the Logicians* (I, 30), 17.
7. Sextus Empiricus, *Outlines of Pyrrhonism* (I, xxxiii), 61.
8. Ibid. (II, vii), 85.
9. Sextus Empiricus, *Against the Logicians* (I, 81), 43.
10. Sextus Empiricus, *Outlines of Scepticism* (II, 10), 69.
11. Sextus Empiricus, *Against the Professors* (III, 40–41), 263/5.
12. For a discussion of the role of the *skandhas* in early Buddhism, see Sue Hamilton, *Early Buddhism: A New Approach, The I of the Beholder* (Richmond, Surrey: Curzon, 2000), especially chapter 3, 143–67.
13. Sextus Empiricus, *Outlines of Scepticism* (III, 254), 209–10; cf. (II, 8), 68.
14. Sextus Empiricus, *Against the Logicians* (II, 187–88), 335/7.
15. Ludwig Wittgenstein, *On Certainty*, trans. G. E. M. Anscombe and G. H. von Wright (New York: Harper and Row, 1972), no. 115, 18e; cf. no. 341, 44e:

"the *questions* that we raise and our *doubts* depend on the fact that some propositions are exempt from doubt, are as it were like hinges on which those turn."

16. Sextus Empiricus, *Outlines of Scepticism*, (I, x), 8.

17. Sextus Empiricus, *Against the Logicians* (I, 89–91), 47–49.

18. Nāgārjuna, *Mūlamadhyamakakārikā* (trans. Garfield), XVIII, 8, 49.

19. Ibid., 250.

20. Ibid., 75.

21. Sextus Empiricus, *Against the Logicians* (I, 343–45), 181/3.

22. Ibid. (I, 358), 189.

23. In my book, *The Soul* (New York: Peter Lang Publishing, 1994), I explore this logic of appearances, which I call the logic of representation and contrast; cf. 21–42.

24. Sextus Empiricus, *Against the Logicians* (I, 409–10), 219.

25. Cf. Ibid. (I, 81), 43.

26. The example of the absence of one "sense" precluding its availability is captured by Sextus in the image of a person born blind and so unable otherwise to achieve sight; he brings it up variously; see, e.g., *Outlines* (III, 49), 156; *Against the Logicians* (I, 55), 29; *Against the Ethicists* (238, 247), 505; and *Against the Professors* (I, 334), 21; see also M. von Senden, *Space and Sight: The Perception of Space and Shape in the Congenitally Blind Before and After Operation*, trans. Peter Heath (Glencoe, Ill.: The Free Press, 1960), *et passim*.

27. George Berkeley, *A Treatise Concerning the Principles of Human Knowledge*, part I, sec. 1, in *Principles, Dialogues, and Philosophical Correspondence*, ed. Colin Murray Turbayne (New York: Bobbs-Merrill, 1965), 22.

28. Here I follow the discussion of Vasubandhu's *Trisvabhāvanirdeśa* by C. W. Huntington, Jr., in his *The Emptiness of Emptiness: An Introduction to Early Indian Madhyamaka* (Honolulu: University of Hawaii Press, 1989), 60–67.

29. Sextus Empiricus, *Against the Ethicists* (87–88), 429.

30. Sextus Empiricus, *Against the Logicians* (I, 361), 191.

31. Cf. Sextus Empiricus, *Outlines of Scepticism* (I, 22), 9, where he says that appearances "depend on passive and unwilled feelings."

32. Ibid. (I, 79), 22.

33. Ibid. (II, 29), 75.

34. Ibid. (II, 72), 85.

35. Sextus Empiricus, *Against the Logicians* (II, 148), 315.

36. Ibid. (II, 147), 315.

37. Ibid. (II, 146), 313.

38. Ibid. (II, 155), 317; it is interesting that one of the lost works by Sextus is entitled *On the Soul*; cf. *Against the Physicists* (II, 284), 349.

39. Quoted in Gadjin M. Nagao, *Mādhyamika and Yogācāra* (Albany: State University of New York Press, 1991), 215.

40. See Leonard C. D. C. Priestley, *Pudgalavāda Buddhism: The Reality of the Indeterminate Self* (Toronto: University of Toronto, Center for South Asian Studies, 1999), 194–95, et passim.

41. Ibid. (II, 151), 315.

42. Sextus Empiricus, *Outlines of Scepticism* (II, 100), 92–93.

43. Ibid. (II, 101), 93.

44. Ibid. (II, 102), 93.

45. Sextus Empiricus, *Against the Logicians* (II, 158), 319.

46. Nāgārjuna, *Mūlamadhyamakakārikā* (trans. Garfield), XXII, 11, 61.

47. Ludwig Wittgenstein, *Tractatus Logico-Philosophicus* (London: Routledge and. Kegan Paul, 1961), 6.54–57, 151.

48. Sextus Empiricus, *Outlines of Scepticism* (I, 31), 11.

49. Sextus Empiricus, *Against the Professors* (II, 97–99), 235/7.

50. Sextus Empiricus, *Outlines of Scepticism* (I, 36–37), 13.

51. Ibid. (I, 38–39), 13.

52. Sue Hamilton, *Early Buddhism*, 169.

53. Ibid., 153.

54. Ibid., 150.

55. Cf. Ibid., 83.

56. Ibid. (I, 24), 9.

57. Sextus Empiricus, *Against the Ethicists* (162–64), 463.

58. Ibid (165), 465.

59. Ibid (166), 465.

60. Cf. Martha Nussbaum, *The Therapy of Desire: Theory and Practice in Hellenistic Ethics* (Princeton, N.J.: Princeton University Press, 1994), 314.

61. Cf. Diogenes Laertius, *Lives of Eminent Philosophers*, vol. 2, trans. R. D. Hicks (Cambridge, Mass.: Harvard University Press, 2000), ix, 66, 479.

62. Sextus Empiricus, *Against the Logicians* (II, 158), 319.

63. Cf. *The Holy Teaching of Vimalakīrti: A Mahāyāna Scripture*, trans. Robert A. F. Thurman (University Park: The University of Pennsylvania Press, 1976).

64. Sue Hamilton, *Early Buddhism*, 164.

# 4

# Modern Pyrrhonism

Pyrrhonism, if my analysis in the preceding chapters is correct, seems to be the sole Western expression of a kind of nondogmatic soteriological practice found more widely in the East. Pyrrhonism as a tradition has fared poorly in modern times insofar as it has usually been confused, as we have seen, with dogmatic scepticism. Obscured by this confusion, its impact has been muted. Its relative absence as an effective philosophy has arguably diminished the modern Western understanding of human experience. Still, if the Pyrrhonist attitude is a valid one, it is bound to be independently rediscovered, it would seem, and we shall explore some instances of this in this chapter. I argued in the last two chapters that there are close links with Madhyamaka Buddhism and other South Asian traditions, and if we can accept a near congruence of Pyrrhonist with Mahāyāna and particularly Madhyamaka attitudes we might consider that something like Pyrrhonism has reentered Western consciousness with the increasing popularity and spread of Buddhism since the twentieth century. The popular Buddhist critique of attachment (to self, ideas, pleasure, power, money, etc.) closely replicates the Pyrrhonist recommendation to suspend judgment about beliefs. And liberation into *nirvāṇa* may well, as I have suggested, approximate the Pyrrhonist *ataxaria*. But Buddhism, especially in its more detailed and subtle explications, has perhaps not yet fully translated into Western forms of expression, linguistic and cultural. And Buddhist ideas in the West, such as no-self or emptiness, have often been popularized in the negative dogmatic sense we find in Academic scepticism, as denying the existence of something rather than suspending judgment about it. Even further, over the centuries Buddhism has taken on a number of strong dogmatic elements of its own. It has become highly ritualized; indeed, both in the East and in the West modern Buddhism has to a large extent turned into another dogmatic religion, with the noncommittal suspension of judgment by the Buddha over nonevident things now largely obscured by dogmatic presumptions concerning no-self and other doctrines.

The quest to bring Buddhism back to what—from the perspective of this work—we might ironically call its "Pyrrhonist" roots has been undertaken by Stephen Batchelor in a recent work, *Buddhism Without Beliefs*. In reviewing the Four Noble Truths—suffering, its origins, its cessation, and the practices leading to its cessation—Batchelor points out that these truths have gradually been transformed from a practical attitude towards experience into "four propositions of fact to be believed. The first truth becomes: 'Life Is Suffering;' the second: 'The Cause of Suffering Is Craving'—and so on. At precisely this juncture, Buddhism becomes a religion. A Buddhist is someone who believes these four propositions."[1] Batchelor reminds us that the Buddha promulgated no doctrine or belief and that he described himself as a healer rather than a savior. The Four Noble Truths, he says, are not theoretical truths but a set of concrete practices. Batchelor makes no reference to Pyrrhonism in his work, yet he strikes a Pyrrhonist note when he invokes agnosticism as a Western analogue to the suspension of belief practiced by the Buddha. Agnosticism was a word coined in the nineteenth century by T. H. Huxley, a populizer of Darwin's ideas, to indicate a third alternative, a middle path between the extremes of positive and negative dogmatic belief. It echoes the point made long ago by Sextus in the first page of his *Outlines* that Pyrrhonism was a third way, a middle path, to be distinguished from the positive beliefs of the dogmatic philosophers as well as from the negative beliefs of the Academic sceptics. Huxley's invention of agnosticism can be read as a spontaneous rediscovery of Pyrrhonist practice, albeit in a limited realm. The term has largely been confined to suspension of judgment with regard to one question: the existence or nonexistence of God. A thoroughgoing Pyrrhonism, of course, would suspend judgment on *all* questions regarding nonevident things, not just the question of God.

Batchelor point outs that the Buddha himself seems to have held some beliefs about the nonevident. One such belief seems to be his acceptance of reincarnation. Batchelor proposes that Buddhists without beliefs suspend judgment on this point: "It may seem that there are two options: either to believe in rebirth or not. But there is a third alternative: to acknowledge, in all honesty, *I do not know*. We neither have to adopt the literal versions of rebirth presented by religious tradition nor fall into the extreme of regarding death as annihilation."[2]

This is not the place to assess how well Batchelor carries through his program of Buddhism without belief on this and other points. He attempts to rethink a number of Buddhist notions, including emptiness, in light of what he calls agnosticism and what we here would call Pyrrhonism, an approach which brings him close to the attitude of the ancient *Sutta Nipāta* and the Madhyamaka classics of Candrakīrti and Nāgārjuna. "Experience," Batchelor sums up, "cannot be accounted for by simply confining it to a conceptual category. Its ultimate ambiguity is that it is simultaneously knowable *and* unknowable. No matter how well we may know something, to witness its intrinsic freedom impels the humble admission: *'I don't really know it.'* Such unknowing is not the end of the track: the point beyond which thinking can proceed no further. This unknowing is the basis of deep agnosticism. When belief and opinion are suspended, the mind has nowhere to rest. We are free to begin a radically other kind of questioning."[3]

The "deep agnosticism" invoked by Batchelor points in the direction of Pyrrhonism. The fact that his book was even necessary, however, shows how far even modern Buddhism has drifted into dogmatism. The Pyrrhonist attitude remains strange and elusive to the modern ear, even to some who would call themselves Buddhists. The "Pyrrhonism" of the ancient Buddhist texts also remains elusive for most modern readers, and it will take more than Batchelor's slim volume to fully bring it out. The story is much the same with regard to modern Western philosophy, which has remained overwhelmingly dogmatic. Here and there as we shall see, however—in the work of philosophers as diverse as George Berkeley and Ludwig Wittgenstein—important aspects of Pyrrhonism spontaneously resurface. Before considering their work, it is important to examine more closely the story of the reception of the ancient Pyrrhonian texts in the modern West, beginning with the publication in France of Latin translations of Sextus in the sixteenth century, followed by the original Greek texts themselves in the early seventeenth century. We know that the confusion of Pyrrhonism with scepticism continued into modern times down to this day, in spite of the ability of Western philosophers to read the ancient texts for themselves. The modern Western failure to understand the Pyrrhonian texts—there is no other way to put it— remains a curious and important cultural phenomenon. We examined the origin of the confusion of Pyrrhonism and scepticism in antiquity in chapter 1, where we considered some symptoms of that confusion among some leading contemporary scholars and philosophers; then we explored in chapter 2 its affinities with Indian thought, particularly Madhyamaka Buddhism; and then in chapter 3 we considered the fundamental distinction made by Pyrrhonism and Madhyamaka-Mahāyāna Buddhism between the evident and nonevident. It remains in this last chapter to take a closer look at the history of the modern reception of Pyrrhonism. Having done that, and after looking at Pyrrhonist elements in Berkeley and Wittgenstein and others, we will be in a position to hazard some considerations of what sort of future Pyrrhonist practice might yet have, and what it might mean culturally, as well as personally.

—*ᴧᴧᴧ*—

The history of modern Pyrrhonism has largely been written by one man, Richard H. Popkin, in an influential book, *The History of Scepticism From Erasmus to Descartes*,[4] first published in 1960 and subsequently expanded and revised; the most recent edition was published in 2003 under the title *The History of Scepticism From Savonarola to Bayle*. A number of related essays of his are collected together as *The High Road to Pyrrhonism*, published in 1980.[5] Unfortunately Popkin, for all his erudition and scholarship, perpetuates the confusion between Pyrrhonism and scepticism he finds in his modern sources, thus compounding the effect. His work is so influential, however, as the scholarly word on modern Pyrrhonism, that it cannot be ignored. For many readers, including myself years ago in graduate school, the introduction to Pyrrhonism begins with an encounter with Popkin's *History of Scepticism*. In the preface to the early edition I consulted back then, he states quite clearly the distinction between Pyrrhonism and Academic scepticism in language close to that of Sextus himself:

> The Pyrrhonian sceptics tried to avoid committing themselves on any and all questions, even as to whether their arguments were sound. Scepticism for them was an ability, or mental attitude, for opposing evidence both pro and con on any question about what was nonevident, so that one would suspend judgment on the question. This state of mind then led to a state of *ataraxia*, quietude, or unperturbedness, in which the sceptic was no longer concerned or worried about matters beyond appearances. Scepticism was a cure for the disease called Dogmatism or rashness. But, unlike Academic scepticism, which came to a negative dogmatic conclusion from its doubts, Pyrrhonian scepticism made no such assertion, merely saying that scepticism is a purge that eliminates everything including itself. The Pyrrhonist, then, lives undogmatically, following his natural inclinations, the appearances he is aware of, and the laws and customs of his society, without ever committing himself to any judgment about them.[6]

This passage remains unchanged in the most recent version of Popkin's book.[7] It is as succinct a summary of the distinction between

Pyrrhonism and Academic scepticism as one is likely to find. Yet in spite of the fundamental importance of this distinction, especially to the Pyrrhonists, Popkin minimizes it throughout his work and tends on the whole to meld the Pyrrhonian and Academic approaches, as if their differences were less important than what they held in common. Pyrrho is described as someone "not a theoretician but rather a living example of the complete doubter,"[8] as if he were an Academic sceptic. There is no mention of the Indian connection or any serious discussion of Pyrrhonism as a therapeutic practice. Though Pyrrhonists advanced no theories, Popkin describes Pyrrhonism "as a theoretical formulation of scepticism,"[9] which he attributes to Aenesidemus who he describes as having built not on Pyrrho but on the work of the Academic sceptics Arcesilaus and Carneades in developing his famous tropes. The significance of the fundamental difference between suspending judgment and drawing negative conclusions is not brought out; nor does Popkin connect it to Pyrrho. Pyrrho makes his cameo appearance and drops out of the account, leaving only the long shadow of his name. Indeed Popkin's book might more accurately have been titled *The History of Pyrrhonism* insofar as he uses the term Pyrrhonism on nearly every page, even more often, it seems, than the term scepticism. By not clearly and fully distinguishing Pyrrhonism from Academic scepticism, however, Popkin perpetuates the misuse of the term "Pyrrhonism" to indicate no more than a variant of Academic scepticism.

Popkin postulates the methodological unity of Pyrrhoniam and Academic scepticism, as if they understood and used their common arsenal of arguments, designed to flummox their opponents, in the same way. In a passage added to the last edition of *The History of Scepticism*, he writes:

> Since the evidence for any such proposition [that is, one asserting some nonempirical or transempirical claim] would be based, according to the sceptics, on either sense information or reasoning, and both of these sources are unreliable to some degree, and no guaranteed or ultimate criterion of true knowledge exits, or is known, there is always some doubt that any nonempirical or transempirical proposition is absolutely true, and hence constitutes real knowledge. As a result, the Academic sceptics said that nothing is certain.[10]

This is fine for Academic sceptics, but what Popkin does not tell us is that Pyrrhonists did *not* accept the beliefs of the Academics, such as they apparently were, that sense information and reason were unreliable, as we have seen. For Pyrrhonists, it is not "sense information or reasoning" that are unreliable, but rather claims made *about* sensations and thoughts, and *about* our reasoning about them. So when Popkin goes on to tell us that, "building on the type of arguments developed by Arcesilaus and Carneades, Aenesidemus and his successors put together a series of 'tropes,' or ways of proceeding to bring about suspense of judgment,"[11] we should remember that arguments against the reliability of sense information as such (insofar as it is appearance rather than belief about appearance) and reason as such (insofar as it is other than the relations among appearances we can sense or imagine) cannot be included among these tropes, and indeed we have argued that they are not. In fact, the tropes, at least in Sextus, nowhere entail them. Sextus, we have seen, is quite careful to acknowledge that appearances and reasoning about them are exempt from doubt. The Pyrrhonist, it is worth repeating, not only suspends judgments about beliefs but is happy to accept sense experience in its evident, direct, involuntary nature as appearance; he or she is also accepting enough of reason (*logos*) as the relations displayed among such appearances (as in smoke being taken as a reason to conclude, as a sign, that there is fire). One would not learn any of this from Popkin.

Popkin displays considerable ambivalence about the Pyrrhonian tradition, which is to say, the texts of Sextus. In earlier editions of *The History of Scepticism* he tells us rather baldly that "Sextus Empiricus was an obscure and unoriginal Hellenistic writer."[12] In the last edition he is considerably more generous. He tells us in his preface that as a graduate student taking the history of philosophy course from John Herman Randall at Columbia University in the 1940s, he found Sextus to be "amazingly lucid and exciting."[13] But in the body of the text he continues to suppress his original enthusiasm, commenting now only that "Sextus Empiricus is usually portrayed as an obscure and unoriginal Hellenistic writer,"[14] though he notes that "Richard Bett suggests that Sextus was a somewhat original figure."[15] Popkin also displays an ambivalence about what Pyrrhonists mean by "belief" (*dogmata*). Reading the Pyrrhonist texts at face value, as we have seen, tells us that they eschewed all belief, that is, all claims which go beyond what is evident, which assert something nonevident. But Popper instead follows in the footsteps of St. Augustine and the early modern European thinkers who followed Augustine in understanding Sextus to be advocating not a practice or way of life but offering an arsenal of arguments to be raided for use against their religious opponents.

Beginning with Augustine, we find a new "spin" on Pyrrhonism which came to be called fideism: the assumption that Sextus' attacks on nonevident beliefs, extensive and thorough as they were, were exclusively attacks on the use of reason (*logos*) to gain knowledge of things nonevident, thereby leaving room for some kind of nonrational knowledge of the nonevident, particularly knowledge through divine revelation or faith. The only revelation recognized by Pyrrhonists, of course, was the revelation of determinate experience, that is, actual appearances of sensations or thoughts. Revelations vouchsafed to some and not others could only be beliefs for the latter. Popkin perpetuates the modern assumption—at odds with the ancient texts—that Pyrrhonian as well as Academic scepticism both are concerned exclusively with nonevident claims made through reason. The assumption is that reason is the only path to the nonevident, a view Pyrrhonists would likely suspend judgment about. The result, again, is to read the texts of Sextus as if he were an Academic sceptic rather than a Pyrrhonist. Conflating the traditions together, Popkin writes:

> The sceptic, in either the Pyrrhonian or Academic tradition, developed arguments to show or suggest that the evidence, reason, or proof employed as grounds for our various beliefs were not completely satisfactory. Then the sceptics recommended suspense of judgment on the question of whether these beliefs were true. One might, however, still maintain the beliefs, even though all sorts of persuasive factors should not be mistaken for adequate evidence that the belief was true.[16]

Pyrrhonists, if the account given in this work is correct, maintain no beliefs at all. If we take reason, as most mainstream ancient and modern thinkers have done, as exclusively a process of abstraction from particulars to universals, then all arguments will be arguments about reason and sceptical conclusions about reason as such will necessarily be sceptical conclusions about all knowledge. This was the approach of the Academic sceptics. And if knowledge of sense perception and imagination is taken to mean knowledge about what our direct and involuntary senses and imaginings represent as obtained by rational inference, then no such knowledge is possible. The Academics made these assumptions, it seems, unlike the Pyrrhonists, and concluded, unlike them, that no knowledge at all was possible. For Academics it would appear that all the tropes were tropes of reason. The Pyrrhonists, by contrast, questioned all sorts of nonevident beliefs, including nonrational ones. We have already noted that Sextus distinguishes between myth, or "acceptance of matters which did not occur and are fictional," and "dogmatic supposition" or "acceptance of a matter which seems to be supported by abduction or proof of some kind, for example, that there are atomic elements of things."[17] It is only the latter that is concerned with reason, or universals; the former, by contrast, is highly particularized, as say our notion of Santa Claus, but no less a belief for all that.

It was St. Augustine who turned Academic scepticism on its head, thus providing the context for the modern misreading of Pyrrhonism. Augustine accepted the Academic nihilist critique of the ancient mainstream schools (Aristotelians, Epicureans, Stoics, Platonists, etc.) with regard to rational knowledge. He concluded that the sceptics showed that pagan philosophy could provide no knowledge of the non-evident, including the divine. He argued instead that knowledge of the nonevident must be nonrational or direct knowledge, such as be-stowed by God through his grace in revelation. In *Contra Academicus*, he argues that this knowledge, which cannot be inferential, must be immediate and direct; that sounds at first like what the Pyrrhonists call an appearance, except this pure knowledge cannot be a sensation or thought, but something beyond them; it is knowledge not of nature but of god. The belief in the divinity of Christ, for instance, could only be for the Pyrrhonists a belief *about* a certain person, one who ap-peared to some people at certain times and places, etc., and who is be-lieved to be divine. The Pyrrhonists, unlike the Academic sceptics, held that appearances—thoughts and sensations—were direct involun-tary modifications of the soul. They did not see thoughts and sensa-tions as form-and-content conceptual packages, but as just what they appeared to be, with nothing "behind them," "causing them," and so on. Augustine, by contrast, follows the Academics in distrusting sen-sations and thoughts and puts in their place a noncorporeal, non-rational intuition, a direct mystical knowledge similar to that pro-pounded by the neo-Platonists, but given instead as a revelation by God through certain historical figures as recounted in the Hebrew and Christian (and later Muslim) scriptures.

As Popkin makes plain, this appeal to a nonrational belief or faith in divine revelation, known as fideism, dominated the minds of those in early modern Christian Europe who encountered the ancient texts on Pyrrhonism. The texts of Sextus in particular began to circulate in manuscript in Italy and Western Europe around the middle of the fif-teenth century; they attracted particular attention in Florence toward the end of that century in the circle around Pico della Mirandola and Savonarola.[18] These figures stand at the head of a long line of mostly fideist thinkers, many of them obscure, who largely defined the con-text in which Sextus was read and misunderstood in the modern West. This is not the place to recapitulate Popkin's account in any detail. What is important is that the ancient Pyrrhonist rejection of *all* belief (if they noticed it) would have been misunderstood and feared by the fideists, who preferred to read Pyrrhonism as a variant of Academic scepticism, indeed as the most extreme version of Academic scepticism: a nihilism in which no beliefs at all were to be admitted. To people obsessed with belief, this must have seemed an incomprehensible position, a kind of *reductio ad absurdum* of belief. Even though they had the text of Sextus in their hands, it seems they were blind to his clear portrayal of Pyrrhonism as a third way, as a nondogmatic way of life, as a door to *ataraxia*. More congenial to them was the Academic outlook that challenged any belief based on reason but did not challenge belief as such (for Academics held at least the belief that knowledge of nonevident things was impossible).

Popkin offers an interesting summary of the fate of this strategy in early modern Europe from the sixteenth to the eighteenth centuries:

> The quest for certainty was to dominate theology and philosophy for the next two centuries, and because of the terrible choice—certainty or total Pyrrhonism—various grandiose schemes of thought were to be constructed to overcome the sceptical crisis. The gradual failure of these monumental efforts was to see the quest for certainty lead to two other searches, the quest for faith—pure fideism—and the quest for reasonableness—or a "mitigated scepticism."[19]

Popkin's capsule summary offers a fair assessment not only of the subsequent history of philosophy in the West, but also of the subsequent history of religion. None of the principal thinkers he considers in detail—Pico della Mirandola, Savonarola, Erasmus, Montaigne, Pierre Charron, Pierre Gassendi, Marin Mersenne, Samuel Sorbiere, Descartes, Pascal, Hobbes, Spinoza, Simon Foucher, and Pierre Bayle, among many others—showed any clear or sustained appreciation of Pyrrhonism as a liberating nondogmatic soteriological practice standing as an alternative to, not a extension of, Academic scepticism. If any of them developed such an appreciation, they kept it to themselves, perhaps out of prudence. Montaigne is typical, praising Pyrrhonism as the summit of human wisdom, but only as a stepping stone to divine revelation. In a passage quoted by Popkin, he states: "There is nothing [other than Pyrrhonism] in man's invention that has so much verisimilitude and usefulness. It presents man naked and empty, acknowledging his natural weakness, fit to receive from above some outside power; stripped of human knowledge, and all the more apt to lodge divine knowledge in himself, annihilating his judgment to make more room for faith . . . a blank tablet prepared to take from the finger of God such forms as he shall be pleased to engrave on it."[20]

Popkin's judgment that modern culture is forced to make a "terrible choice" between "certainty" and "total Pyrrhonism" takes us back to the opening page of Sextus Empiricus' *Outlines*. There Sextus offers the same two choices, but offers a third alternative as well. Though Popkin duly notes this elsewhere, as we have seen, he forgets it here. Sextus and Popkin both acknowledge the dogmatism of positive beliefs. As for the second choice, nihilism, Popkin unfortunately characterizes it as "total Pyrrhonism," meaning, as he says later, that "in a fundamental sense our basic beliefs have no foundation."[21] This is the conclusion that we cannot have knowledge of what we believe, of what is nonevident. This same second choice is described by Sextus in similar language as a "denial of discovery."[22] But for Sextus this second choice is not Pyrrhonism of any sort, but rather Academic scepticism, or negative dogmatism. While these two alternatives seem to exhaust Popkin's considered inventory of possibilities, the whole point of Sextus' work is to introduce a third possibility, namely, Pyrrhonism itself. Popkin's confusion of Pyrrhonism with Academic scepticism is an old story, as we have seen, and here he is mostly at one with the modern thinkers making the same confusion. The difference between Pyrrhonism and Academic scepticism turns out to be for Popkin and the moderns, instead of a profound contrast, a matter of degree.

Sometimes, however, glimmerings of what Sextus was trying to do peek through the fog. In discussing a disciple of Montaigne, Jean Pierre Camus, Popkins dutifully reports as follows: "Rather than rambling through the various themes of Pyrrhonian philosophy, as Montaigne did, or welding them into a battery of arguments, primarily against Aristotelianism, as Charron did, Camus created a vast structure of Hegelian thesis, antithesis, and synthesis. The thesis is Academic scepticism—nothing can be known; the antithesis is dogmatism—something can be known; and the synthesis—'sceptical indifference,' the Pyrrhonian suspense of judgment."[23] This is not the place to explore Camus' work, but it seems that he took the central distinctions laid down by Sextus at least seriously enough to organize his text around them. He perhaps realized consciously that Pyrrhonism is not to be confused with Academic scepticism, that they are radically different from one another. But, as Popkin tells the story, in his very long book Camus spends most of his time discussing Academic scepticism and dogmatism, and devotes only a few disappointing pages at the end to Pyrrhonism, where he suggests that anyone interested in learning more should go and read Sextus.[24] Camus, who ended up a Catholic bishop, was likely not in a position to suspend judgment about Christian beliefs.

Popkin's own sympathies lay with what he calls "the development of 'mitigated scepticism.'" This solution," he tells us, "formulated in embryo by Castellio and Chillingworth, and in detail by Mersenne and Gassendi, was to be further developed by the sceptics Glanvill, Foucher, and, finally, David Hume. They were to show a way by which theoretical Pyrrhonism could be reconciled with our practical means for determining truths adequate for human purposes."[25] "Mitigated or constructive scepticism," he adds elsewhere, "represents a new way, possibly the closest to contemporary empirical and pragmatic methods, of dealing with the abyss of doubt that the crisis of the Reformation and the scientific revolution had opened up. (It was novel for its time, though it obviously echoes some of the attitudes of Greek thinkers like Carneades.)" In the same passage, he goes on to conclude that in mitigated scepticism "the doubts propounded by the Pyrrhonists in no way affected *la verite des sciences*, provided that the sciences were interpreted as hypothetical systems about appearances and not true descriptions of reality, as practical guides to actions and not ultimate information about the true nature of things. *La crise pyrrhonienme* fundamentally could not be resolved, but, at least it could be ignored or abided with, if one could regulate the doubts to the problems of dogmatic philosophy, while pursuing scientific knowledge as the guide to practical living."[26] The Academic sceptical (not Pyrrhonian) notion of probabilistic knowledge (its true source evidenced by the reference to Carneades) is rehabilitated by Popkin as the best we can expect. The negative dogmatic sceptical conclusion that we can't really know anything is given away by Popkin's admission that the crisis of Pyrrhonism "fundamentaly could not be resolved." The hypothetical acceptance of scientific hypotheses was congenial enough to Pyrrhonists, of course, but it was far from the sort of second-best compromise Popkin presents; for them it was part of a fundamental human liberation, a positive release from suffering of which we find almost no appreciation in the modern responses to Pyrrhonism.

—⟨∿∿⟩—

At least one early modern philosopher broke through the barrier, at least in part, which has confined Western thinkers to the alternatives of positive dogmatism and Academic scepticism. That philosopher was George Berkeley, the Anglo-Irish bishop of the eighteenth century famous for his provocative denial of the existence of the external world, and the author of some of the most lucid philosophical prose written in the English language. Berkeley occupies a secure niche in the pantheon of Western philosophers, where he is commonly presented as the middle term of the Locke-Berkeley-Hume trio of British empiricists. I suggest a different reading of his work. Unlike Locke the positive dogmatist and Hume the Academic sceptic, Berkeley saw no reason to continue to suppose that some kind of independently existing external reality somehow has to underlay our appearances. He broke with the mainstream philosophical tradition and its fundamental distinction between appearance and reality. Berkeley was an Anglican churchman who eventually became Bishop of Cloyne in Ireland; he was a man of faith, and therefore no Pyrrhonist. Yet he adopted most of the more radical conclusions reached by ancient Pyrrhonists. Like them, and perhaps uniquely among influential modern philosophers, he denied the distinction between reality and appearance by obliterating it: appearances, he boldly stated, *were* reality, or as he famously put it in his major work, the *Principles of Human Knowledge*, "*esse* is *percipi*," to be is to be perceived, or as the ancient Pyrrhonists might have put it, to be is to be self-evident to a consciousness or soul.[27]

Virtually all philosophers, ancient and modern, with the exception of the Pyrrhonists, have distrusted our immediately evident thoughts and sensations and decried them as so many unreal illusions, while insisting that what is real must be something else, something nonevident. Berkeley, by contrast, boldly affirms that immediately evident thoughts and sensations are entirely real, and that their reality consists in their being perceived by some consciousness, which he calls "spirit." Thoughts and sensations for Berkeley, as for ancient Pyrrhonists, are objects of consciousness, while spirits (the Pyrrhonists speak of "soul") are subjects of consciousness. With this move, the postulation of any reality existing independently of being perceived becomes not only unnecessary, but also implausible. In his *Three Dialogues Between Hylas and Philonous* Berkeley sums up his philosophy as follows: "My endeavors tend only to unite and place in a clearer light that truth which was before shared between the vulgar and the philosophers, for former being of opinion that *those things they immediately perceive are the real things*, and the latter, that *the things immediately perceived are ideas which exist only in the mind*. Which two notions put together do, in effect, constitute the substance of what I advance."[28]

It was plain to Berkeley that belief in nonevident realities led to scepticism of the Academic variety, that is, the conclusion that such nonevident realities could not be known. In the Preface to his *Three Dialogues Between Hylas and Philonous*, he states that "Upon the common principles of philosophers we are not assured of the existence of things from their being perceived. And we are taught to distinguish their real nature from that which falls under our senses. Hence arise skepticism and paradoxes."[29] In his roughly written early notebooks, published as *Philosophical Commentaries*, he writes in his abbreviated style that "many of the Ancient philosophers run into so great absurdity as even to deny the existence of motion and those other things they perceiv'd actually by their senses, this sprung from their not knowing wt existence was and where it consisted this is the source of their Folly, 'tis on the discovering of the nature & meaning & import of existence that I chiefly insist. This puts a wide difference between the Sceptics & me. This I think wholly new. I am sure 'tis new to me."[30] In another entry, he writes: "Twas the opinion that Ideas could exist unperceiv'd or before perception that made Men think perception was somewhat different from the Idea perceived, yt it was an Idea of Reflexion whereas the thing perceiv'd was an idea of Sensation. I say twas this made 'em think the understanding took it in receiv'd it from without wch could never be did not they think it existed without."[31] And as far as "ideas" (his term for appearances) are concerned, Berkeley writes in the notebooks that "By Idea I mean any sensible or imaginable thing."[32]

If Berkeley had read Sextus (as he might have, though there seems to be no direct evidence he did), he would have discovered there his own thesis, namely, the notion that appearances have what reality they have for us by virtue of being perceived, that is, they exist for us insofar as they are modifications of the soul, or consciousness, and not (as far as we can tell) because they are the manifestations of some other reality. It seems that Berkeley came to his conclusions independently, though he likely was stimulated by his reading of sceptical modern philosophers, especially Pierre Bayle (1647–1706).[33] A French Huguenot, though briefly a Catholic in his youth, Bayle's most famous work was his *Dictionnaire historique et critique* (1696), an encyclopedically organized monster work of more than seven million words; one of the most important entries is his article "Pyrrho."[34] Bayle seems not to have advanced any views of his own; indeed, he specialized in developing mutually-cancelling arguments in the Pyrrhonian spirit. Tip-toeing through the treacherous landscape of post-Reformation Christian religious controversy, Bayle seems to have practiced a kind of Pyrrhonism resulting in suspension of judgment as a practical matter, implying in the end that God, if there is a God, remains indeterminate and beyond characterization. On the other hand, he appears to have accepted (or at least not opposed) Augustinian fideism, the notion that arguments against nonevident beliefs open some kind of door to faith. Unlike dogmatic polemicists seeking to demolish one dogma in favor of another, however, his relentless Pyrrhonian criticisms of any attempt to determine the nature of any such faith—though he avoided criticizing New Testament doctrines too directly—only served to suggest that faith could have no content, an outcome not congenial to Augustine and Christian theology. He flirts with recognizing the sort of practical liberation invoked by Pyrrhonists, but nowhere seems to make it explicit.[35] He too, though, falls short of full Pyrrhonism, as is made plain by his article "Pyrrho." There he tells us that "His [Pyrrho's] views were hardly different from those of Arcesilaus."[36] He adds that even though "one relizes that this logic [of Sextus Empiricus] is the greatest effort of subtlety that the human mind has been able to accomplish," he immediately concludes, "But, at the same time, one sees that this subtlety is in no way satisfactory."[37] Where does Bayle end up? He is clear enough in the end: "The natural conclusion of this ought to be to renounce this guide [reason] and to implore the cause of all things to give us a better one. This is a great step to the Christian religion."[38]

Bayle was more relentless in his critique of natural science, or rather the metaphysics thereof, than of religion. Early modern philosophers cast the distinction between reality and appearance as a distinction between primary and secondary qualities. Primary qualities are said to be those nonevident, abstract, mathematical entities underlying objects—mainly extension, and its manifestations in space, time, motion, etc.—while secondary qualities are said to be those evident, concrete entities we actually sense and imagine, such as colors, shapes, sounds, touches, etc. Secondary qualities are said to be our immediate perceptions, what we directly experience or feel subjectively, while primary qualities are said to be mediate inferences to enduring abstract realities lying behind our fleeting, changing, and unreliable immediate perceptions. It was the business of science, most early modern philosophers thought, to discover the defining primary qualities of our experience, which constituted knowledge, as opposed to the chaotic uncertainty of direct experience. Berkeley took arguments against this distinction from Bayle and others (most if not all of them traceable back to Sextus) and, adding some new supporting evidence,[39] wrought a devastating critique of the purported "reality" of primary qualities, leaving no basis for any belief in their independent, external existence. As he puts it in the *Principles*:

> They who assert that figure, motion, and the rest of the primary or original qualities do exist without the mind in unthinking substances

do at the same time acknowledge that colors, sounds, heat, cold, and suchlike secondary qualities do not—which they tell us are sensations existing in the mind alone, that depend on and are occasioned by the different size, texture, and motion of the minute particles of matter. This they take for an undoubted truth which they can demonstrate beyond all exception. Now, if it be certain that those original qualities are inseparably united with the other sensible qualities, and not, even in thought, capable of being abstracted from them, it plainly follows that they exist only in the mind. But I desire anyone to reflect and try whether he can, by any abstraction of thought, conceive the extension and motion of a body without all other sensible qualities. For my own part, I see evidently that it is not in my power to frame an idea of a body extended and moved, but I must withal give it some color or other sensible quality which is acknowledged to exist only in the mind. In short, extension, figure, and motion, abstracted from all other qualities, are inconceivable. Where therefore the other sensible qualities are, there must these be also, to wit, in the mind and nowhere else.[40]

The cause of this erroneous belief that "houses, mountains, rivers, and in a word, all sensible objects have an existence, natural or real, distinct from their being perceived by the understanding," Berkeley tells us, will "be found at bottom to depend on the doctrine of abstract ideas."[41] He gives numerous examples of this doctrine, which he nevertheless finds incomprehensible. One is said to be able to abstract from numerous particulars to a general or abstract conclusion, thus taking particular men such as Peter, James, and John, and many others, tall and short, dark and light, thin and fat, and so on, and dispensing with the distinguishing qualities of each and retaining only the common qualities, and so arriving at a abstract form or essence of man. Or one is said to be able to abstract from the different types of triangle, such as equilateral, isosceles, right, etc., and arrive at an abstract idea of triangle as such. And so on. Berkeley's point—the same as that made by the ancient Pyrrhonists—is that no such abstract entities can be produced in sense or even imagined, and that anything we can perceive is one or another specific thing, a particular man, say Peter or James, not "man in general." There is no warrant for concluding that such abstractions in any way represent independently existing objects lying beyond and informing the particular things we actually perceive.

Berkeley also echoes the Pyrrhonist view of signification when he argues that language is the source of the notion of abstraction, particularly the presumption that "every name has, or ought to have, one only precise and settled signification, which inclines men to think there are certain abstract, determinate ideas which constitute the true and only immediate signification of each general name."[42] Because I can freely use the word "man" as easily as I can use the words "Peter" and "James," it seems that there must be something definite corresponding to "man" just as there is something definite corresponding to the names of our friends "Peter" and "James." This closely parallels Sextus' point that for dogmatists indicative signs, such as the word "soul," are presumed to stand for something definite, just as commemorative or recollective signs such as "smoke" and "fire" do in fact stand for something, even though no such definite things can be produced in the former case as they can be in the latter.[43] Berkeley, like Sextus, has no use for such indicative abstract signs. Words can indeed be made general, but only as particulars standing for other particulars, not as particulars standing for abstractions. In considering whether we need a general abstract idea of a triangle, Berkeley tells us that "though the idea I have in view whilst I make the demonstration be, for instance, that of an isoceles rectangular triangle whose sides are of a determinate length, I may nevertheless be certain it extends to all other rectilinear triangles, of what sort of bigness soever. And that because neither the right angle, nor the equality, nor determinate length of the sides are at all concerned in the demonstration. It is true the diagram I have in view includes all these particulars, but then there is not the least mention made of them in the proof of the proposition."[44]

For Berkeley, as for Sextus, appearances or perceptions are particulars, that is, definite objects of consciousness of one sort or another. Although objects of consciousness are subject to change—Peter, James, and John change as they grow older, perhaps dramatically so if they are injured, and one day they will die and their bodies will be destroyed—this does not mean that appearances cannot also endure in some commonly recognizable if limited way. Usually I can rely on the fact that the Peter, James, and John I saw yesterday can be seen tomorrow. And some objects—an ounce of gold, say, or a molecule of water—might endure with no apparent change indefinitely. The notion that the being of such objects for us lies in their being perceived—that their *esse* is *percipi*—echoes the correlation between objects and consciousness found in Sextus. In Sextus appearances are modifications of the soul, just as they are for Berkeley. And as we suffer appearances passively in Sextus, just so in Berkeley our perceptions are passive not active.[45] For Berkeley, it is spirit or consciousness or soul which is active, that is, energy unbound, while the objects of consciousness are in themselves passive, as in Sextus; that is, they are energy bound and stabilized rather than unbound and released: "A spirit is one simple, undivided, active being—as it perceives ideas it is called 'the understanding,' and as it produces or otherwise operates about them it is called 'the will.' Hence there can be no idea formed of a soul or spirit; for all ideas whatever, being passive and inert, they cannot represent unto us, by way of image or likeness, that which acts."[46]

The fact that "there can be no idea formed of soul or spirit" suggests that whatever spirit may be it must necessarily be indeterminate. Spirit cannot be identified with any of the ideas it entertains, and so cannot be characterized, it would seem, in any way, just as the ancient Pyrrhonists consistently maintained. Having reached this conclusion, however, Berkeley then part ways with the ancient Pyrrhonists. He proclaims, particularly in his sermons and other non-philosophical writings, a strong faith in Christian revelation, proclaims Jesus as his Savior, and generally accepts and propounds the characterizations of the nonevident divinity found in Christian scripture. In a sermon on "The Will of God," Berkeley writes that "the will of God is declared unto us in a twofold manner, by the light of reason and by revelation."[47] The light of reason is a path to insight, but not an easy one: "the Gentiles [ancient pagans] might by a due use of their reason," he tells us in another sermon, "by thought and study, observing the beauty and order of the world, and the excellency and profitableness of vertue, have obtained some sense of a Providence and of Religion; . . . But how few were they who made this use of their reason, or lived according to it!"[48] Berkeley's own philosophical works are presumably contributions to the method of the light of reason. "But, as the light of reason is often obscured," he also informs us, "& impressions on the conscience defaced through indolence and neglect, through custom prejudice and passion: therefore the will of God hath been promulgated, by the preaching and miracles of our blessed Saviour and his apostles."[49]

Even without invoking revelation, Berkeley goes beyond what Pyrrhonists would allow to infer the spirit of God from our experience of the objects of consciousness. If objects have their being by being perceived, the question arises about what being objects have when there is no one to perceive them. "The table I write on I say exists," Berkeley explains, "that is, I see and feel it; and if I were out of my study I should say it existed—meaning thereby that if I was in my study I might perceive it, or that some other spirit actually does perceive it."[50] Berkeley has turned into a necessary connection what the ancient Pyrrhonists would say was in experience no more than an unfailingly consistent association between ideas and spirits. To say that *esse* is *percipi* is to go beyond the apparent correlation of appearances with consciousness made by Sextus to conclude with a general belief that to be is to be perceived. The same difficulty arises with his claim that the objects we involuntarily perceive (no less than nature itself) must be evidence of a larger spirit, of some other will than ours: "When in broad daylight I open my eyes, it is not in my power to choose whether I shall see or no, or to determine what particular objects shall present themselves to my view; and so likewise as to the hearing and the other senses; the ideas imprinted on them are not creatures of my will. There is therefore some other will that produces them."[51] Or as he puts it more bluntly: "The ideas of sense are more strong, lively, and distinct than those of the imagination; they have likewise a steadiness, order, and coherence, and are not excited at random, as those which are the effects of human wills often are, but in a regular train or series, the admirable connection whereof sufficiently testifies the wisdom and benevolence of its Author."[52] Instead of concluding the existence of a divine author behind phenomena, ancient Pyrrhonists would have suspended judgment.

Although Berkeley, almost alone among modern philosophers, reached (probably via Bayle) some of the conclusions drawn by ancient Pyrrhonists, he seems not to have developed any kind of philosophical practice along the lines of the Pyrrhonists.[53] Instead he gave his conclusions a dogmatic turn (following Augustine, as did Bayle) as arguments for Christian revelation. Berkeley nevertheless struck what has probably been the most remarkable blow in modern Western philosophy in favor of a key Pyrrhonist point, namely, the dependent reality (what the Buddhists call dependent origination) of appearances, which he called ideas. That he fell into dogmatism in conclusions drawn from this point, and advanced as an inference worthy of belief the reality of the author of nature, or God, makes his contribution no less remarkable. His arguments on consciousness-dependent ideas have not, however, proved persuasive, compelling as they are; they have continued to baffle and perplex subsequent philosophers, who have laughed them off rather than refuted them, in the spirit of Dr. Johnson's attempt to refute Berkeley by kicking a stone. The tone for modern philosophers on Berkeley was set by Hume, in a footnote in his *Enquiry*, where he describes him as an "ingenious author" whose arguments *"admit of no answer and produce no conviction. Their only effect is to cause that momentary amazement and irresolution and confusion, which is the result of scepticism."*[54] Hume, of course, was the sceptic, not Berkeley, and it seems that, confronted with Berkeley's arguments, he could not imagine him otherwise. Modern Western philosophy has continued to hold the distinction between appearance and reality and to advance, to the point of exhaustion, one theory after another to attempt to substantiate the distinction, while one sceptical attack after another has struck down each in turn. Berkeley may have been a dogmatist about spirit (asserting its incarnation through Jesus Christ), but his arguments against matter (the independent existence of objects in the external world) have remained unanswered in modern Western philosophy.

—⁓⁓—

Perhaps the only major modern Western philosopher not only to rediscover independently something like a Pyrrhonist attitude toward experience but also to come close to realizing it as a practical philosophy in the ancient sense was Ludwig Wittgenstein. Wittgenstein was notorious in his disregard for the history of philosophy, and poorly read in it; it is doubtful he had any firsthand knowledge of the ancient Pyrrhonist texts.[55] Nonetheless, almost untrammeled by dogmatic conviction and naturally resistant to the attitude we call Academic scepticism, Wittgenstein developed something very like the philosophical practice of the ancient Pyrrhonists. It's a pity he seems not to have known their work. The son of a wealthy, assimilated Jewish Viennese family, Wittgenstein grew up in pre–World War I Austria. An early interest in engineering and mathematics led him to study in England. He eventually made his way to Cambridge, where he became a protégé of Bertrand Russell. He returned to Austria to fight in World War I. During and after the war he developed his ideas in a work, the *Tractatus Logico-Philosophicus*, which was published in 1921, with Russell's help. The work quickly became something of a cult classic among positivist philosophers. Wittgenstein, though, felt it was misunderstood and, despairing of professional philosophy, he returned to Austria and for some years led a relatively obscure life as a secondary school teacher. Eventually he returned to philosophical circles, ending up once more at Cambridge, where he further developed his ideas, although in a somewhat different, more diffused style. He published little in his lifetime apart from the *Tractatus*, though some of his later work was published shortly after his death under the title *Philosophical Investigations*, and numerous other shorter works have since been published.

In spite of the fame he achieved and the following he attracted during his lifetime, Wittgenstein continued to despair over the reception of his work, which he feared was not well understood. His focus in his early work was the logical foundations of mathematics, and in his later work it shifted to various modes of representation in language, which he called "language games." Common to both, however, was a deep interest in representation or depiction, that is, in what could be represented and what could not. Here we can see some parallels with ancient Pyrrhonism emerging. Wittgenstein was deeply sceptical of what he regarded as bogus claims often made about various aspects of experience, what we might call nonevident claims about experience. In the preface to his *Tractatus*, he says: "The whole sense of the book might be summed up in the following words: what can be said at all can be said clearly, and what we cannot talk about we must pass over in silence."[56] What can be said at all is no more or less than some account of facts to be found in the world, and these facts are made up of objects variously related to one another: "What is the case—a fact—is the existence of states of affairs."[57] The objects that make up facts, or states of affairs, are defined by the various roles they play in defining different facts.

Wittgenstein, I shall argue, is in effect a fully Pyrrhonian philosopher. Like the Pyrrhonists he does not doubt appearances, but takes them as his criteria. Let us begin with what he says about appearances, or objects, as he calls them. Objects for Wittgenstein exist, as they do for ancient Pyrrhonists, only in relation to other objects; they have their being in what Buddhists call "dependent origination." A "table" is something that might variously stand in my study, be made by a carpenter, have value as an antique, be chopped up for firewood, etc. Almost anything might be a table in certain circumstances, e.g., a tree stump in the forest might be a table for a picnic. And so on. Objects are the familiar stuff of appearances—our sensations and thoughts—as we have discussed throughout. A particular object—say the maple tree in front of my house—is subject to change from one day to the next and has a limited existence, yet it also retains a great deal of enduring integrity from day to day, enough to make it more or less recognizably the same tree from day to day. This tree is a bundle of visual, tactile, audible, olfactory, and gustatory appearances (as Berkeley points out).[58] Wittgenstein, like the ancient Pyrrhonists and Berkeley, can find no reason to doubt these objects of experience. In a later work, *On Certainty*, he points out that: "The game of doubting itself presupposes certainty."[59] He amplifies the point a bit later: "How do I know that this color is blue? If I don't trust *myself* here, why should I trust anyone else's judgment? Is there a why? Must I not begin to trust somewhere? That is to say: somewhere I must begin with not-doubting; and that is not, so to speak, hasty but excusable: it is part of judging."[60]

The ancient Pyrrhonists were interested in inquiry, in seeking the answers to puzzling questions. Now inquiry presupposes doubt. If we have no doubt about something it would not occur to us to inquire about it. Wittgenstein points out that doubt itself presupposes certainty. We can doubt something only against a background of certainty. Wittgenstein gives the example of a schoolboy who asks his teacher: "'and is there a table there even when I turn round, and even when *no one* is there to see it?' . . . Perhaps the teacher will get a bit impatient," Wittgenstein adds, "but think that the boy will grow out of asking such questions. That is to say, the teacher will feel that this is not really a legitimate question at all. And it would be just the same if the pupil cast doubt on the uniformity of nature, that is to say on the justification of inductive arguments.—The teacher would feel that this was only holding them up, and this way the pupil would only get stuck and make no progress.—And he would be right. It would be as if someone were looking for some object in a room; he opens a drawer and doesn't see it there; then he closes it again, waits, and opens it once more to see if perhaps it isn't there now, and keep on like that. He has not learned to look for things. And in the same way this pupil has not learned how to ask questions. He has not learned the game that we are trying to teach him."[61]

Wittgenstein again and again points out that complete or total doubt, the doubt of the Academic sceptics, is incoherent: "the *questions* that we raise and our *doubts* depend on the fact that some propositions are exempt from doubt, are as it were like hinges on which those turn. . . . If we want the door to turn, the hinges must stay put."[62] And later, very succinctly: "A doubt that doubted everything would not be a doubt."[63] In the *Tractatus* he tells us that "Scepticism is not irrefutable, but obviously nonsensical, when it tries to raise doubts where no questions can be asked. For doubt can exist only where a questions exists, a question only where an answer exists, and an answer only where something can be *said*."[64] What can be said is an empirical or factual matter, a matter of appearances. We might be wrong about this or that appearance, but being wrong about this or that appearance only makes sense insofar as we are right about other appearances, or objects.

Wittgenstein points out that we posit names corresponding to objects, and that a certain grouping of names reflects a corresponding grouping of objects: "A name names an object. The object is its meaning. . . . The configuration of objects in a situation corresponds to the configuration of simple signs in the propositional sign."[65] This is Wittgenstein's famous "picture theory" of meaning whereby he holds that sensical language is language in which names are put into a relationship which mirrors a relationship in which their corresponding objects stand to one another. The names and the objects named are usually very different from one another (e.g., the musical notes we hear and the printed notes we see in a musical score), yet the patterning displayed by the relationship of the names (the sequence of printed notes on the printed musical staff) displays a point by point correspondence with the actual notes played by musicians in the corresponding piece of music. Similarly, of course, the names in language are very different from the objects named (the word "cat" is very different from a cat), yet a certain combination of names ("the cat is on the mat") literally pictures a certain state of affairs among the corresponding objects.

This relationship between signs and things signified is essentially the same as that advocated by Sextus in his account of commemorative or recollective signs and the appearances they signify, though Wittgenstein provides a detailed exposition lacking in Sextus. And just as Sextus rejects the claims of dogmatists for indicative signs, that is, for signs purported to represent nonappearances or nonevident things, just so Wittgenstein rejects the claims of contemporary philosophers and indeed of common usage insofar as it presumes that we also have names and propositions which indicate nonevident things, which Wittgenstein calls "nonsense." "Propositions," Wittgenstein writes, "can represent the whole of reality, but they cannot represent what they must have in common with reality in order to be able to represent it—logical form."[66] Paul Engelmann, Wittgenstein's friend and one of the most useful commentators on his work, puts the point as follows: "An image, a picture, can represent anything except its own representational relationship to the depicted subject. (The rays of projection from the points of the original to those of the image cannot themselves appear in the picture.) If, then, the true propositions form a picture of the world, they can say nothing about their own relation to the world, by virtue of which they are its picture."[67] The relationship between the world (appearances) and language (representation, depiction) is logic, or logical form, and this is precisely what, according to Wittgenstein, cannot be represented.

For the ancient Pyrrhonists, nonevident claims about the world could neither be affirmed nor denied; instead judgment about them was to be suspended. These claims, they said, anticipating Wittgenstein, resulted from the misuse of language to try to represent what cannot be represented. As Sextus puts it: "Pyrrhonists do not assent to anything unclear."[68] Wittgenstein uses almost the same language: "Without philosophy thoughts are, as it were, cloudy and indistinct; its task is to make them clear and to give them sharp boundaries."[69] Sextus achieves clarity by ruling out through questioning and examination individual dogmatic claims made by others; he offers no systematic sense, however, of how it is that others come to make such claims, or even whether they have anything in common beyond the lack of clarity. This is precisely what Wittgenstein attempted in the *Tractatus*, where the consistent theme is that unclarity comes from the misbegotten effort to say (depict) what cannot be said (depicted). Now one of the assumptions of the *Tractatus* was that there was an overall general logical form to all representation or depiction, and that this form included language as well. It seems that Wittgenstein at that time continued under the spell of Russell's program of reducing language to logic. At some point in the 1920s, when he was not active in philosophical circles, he seems to have concluded that no such overall general logical form could be assumed. His later philosophy emphasizes the apparent irreducible diversity of logical forms, the variety of which he called "grammars" or "language games," each with its own direct and unique manner of representing (or misrepresenting) the world. This gives Wittgenstein's later work a diffused and somewhat fragmented character, with problems being posed from a variety of disparate sources; the result, interestingly, is a style much closer to Sextus than to the *Tractatus*.

Each such language game, however, if it is to be clear and not nonsensical, is still a matter of some kind of correspondence between some kind of representation and some state of affairs. The need for a correspondence between signification and things signified is already established in Sextus' insistence on commemorative or recollective signs, as opposed to the indicative signs of the dogmatists where such a correspondence cannot be established. Wittgenstein's notion of representation or depiction in effect fleshes out this Pyrrhonian insight. If we understand an object to be both a part and a whole, we can begin to appreciate Wittgenstein's contribution. As a part, an object plays a role in a variety of larger wholes or contexts (as in the example of the table above); as a whole an object contains its own parts or internal relations, without which it would have no integrity, and could not be a part in any larger whole. So any object is defined by the parts that comprise it as well as the wholes of which it is a part. Any depiction (description, representation, etc.) is itself an object, that is, a whole (a memory, a picture, a narrative, a musical score) that displays some configuration of parts (thoughts, colors, words, notes). It will represent some other object insofar as its parts are configured in the same way as the parts of the other object. The representation reproduces in one object (the representation) certain relationships, or forms, displayed by another object (the object represented).[70]

Wittgenstein makes the point that the forms displayed by any object can be displayed, or shown, by another object through representation, but those forms cannot *themselves* be displayed or shown *without* the parts which display them. The form of any object is the
configuration of its parts, and it can be reproduced only by the same
configuration of parts in another object. The configuration itself cannot be separated from the parts that display it; it has no independent
existence. In this basic sense, forms are nonevident. Wittgenstein argues that there is something nonevident *within* appearances, namely,
the forms each of them as objects display. When the Pyrrhonists suspend judgment about the nonevident, they do not dismiss it, as dogmatic sceptics would. They rather point out that the nonevident is indeterminate, and that we can make no judgments about what is
indeterminate. When they say that the nonevident cannot be shown to
exist, and might not exist, they are telling us that it cannot be shown
to *exist as an object* or independent entity of any sort. It is not something that we can represent or describe in language, or any other
medium of representation, but neither can we conclude that it is nothing at all. Wittgenstein says the same thing about the forms of objects.
They too are indeterminate, incapable of description. He insists, however, that the indeterminate in this case exists not independently of
appearances, but is rather intrinsic to them as their form. If Sextus can
be read, or misread, as presuming that the nonevident is necessarily
somehow outside of appearances, Wittgenstein forestalls any such
misreading by showing us how the nonevident can also be understood
to be within appearances. It is only the conceit of the dogmatists, who
create a separate, fictitious realm of existence, which insists upon separating the nonevident from the evident.

This helps to explain the Pyrrhonist attitude toward experience so
puzzling to most commentators. If we assume that suspension of judgment about the nonevident is a suspension of judgment about one
sort of thing (the nonevident) while judgments continue to be made
about another sort of thing (the evident), then the indeterminate is
presumed to be in some kind of separate realm. But if we recall that
appearances at least for us are appearances to a soul or spirit or consciousness (as Berkeley insisted), then the indeterminate and the determinate somehow come together. For Wittgenstein the forms displayed by objects were the most important thing about them; although
these forms were indeterminate or ineffable, they were, he maintained, what affected us the most. If we agree with Sextus that an appearance is an involuntary modification of the soul, we can find in

Wittgenstein a demonstration that this is a function of the forms displayed by (or within) appearances. Although forms can be *shown*, as Wittgenstein famously puts it, they cannot be *said*, that is, they cannot be distinguished as objects in their own right from the objects that display them. Just as I cannot find my "self" as one object among the objects of my consciousness, so I cannot find "truth" or "beauty" or "justice" or any other nonevident things as objects among the objects of my consciousness. As Wittgenstein put it in a letter to his Austrian publisher, trying to elucidate the *Tractatus*:

> *The book's point is an ethical one.* I once meant to include in the preface a sentence which is not in fact there now, but which I will write out for you here, because it will perhaps be a key to the work for you. What I meant to write, then, was this: My work consists of two parts: the one presented here plus all that I have *not* written. And *it is precisely this second part that is the important one.* My book draws limits to the sphere of the ethical from the inside as it were, and I am convinced that this is the ONLY rigorous way of drawing those limits. In short, I believe that where many others today are just *gassing*, I have managed in my book to put everything firmly into place by being silent about it.[71]

Our experience of appearances cannot be reduced to a description of those appearances, in contrast to the claims of the logical positivists of Wittgenstein's time, and most other empirically and scientifically-oriented modern philosophers to this day. Both an experience and a description of that experience contain, according to Wittgenstein, something that cannot be described, something ineffable that nonetheless is somehow shown both through the experience and through its description. This ineffable form constitutes for Wittgenstein the value of the experience—its involuntary effect, as it were. If we value a work of art, say a painting or musical performance, or some natural experience, perhaps a bucolic view, or human behavior such as a moral act, it is because of the intangible quality of the indescribable form displayed by that experience. To hearken back to Sextus' endorsement of "everyday observances" including "guidance by nature, necessitation by feelings, handing down of laws and customs, and teaching of kinds of expertise," we can perhaps appreciate more fully in light of Wittgenstein that these need not be understood as transparently bare facts merely prompting one or another physical reaction, but rather as affect-laden appearances whose ineffable forms pack an emotional charge, whether positive, negative, or neutral. A nondogmatic life is a full life, one in which the Pyrrhonist, freed of distorting dogmatic illusions, can engage with experience directly and fully.

—⁊⁊⁊—

We may conclude with some conjectures on the future of Pyrrhonism. What are the possibilities in our time for living a nondogmatic life, a life without belief? If the arguments presented in this book concerning Pyrrhonism have any validity, it would seem that the only alternative to one or another type of dogmatism, positive or negative, is to adopt something like the Pyrrhonist attitude to experience. This Pyrrhonist attitude is akin, I have suggested, to the middle path of Buddhism. Pyrrhonism, ancient and modern, was intended by those who understood and practiced it as a serious way of life. Wittgenstein's friend Paul Engelmann describes Wittgenstein's philosophy as a practical method of living, one that he called "wordless faith" which he understood as nothing less than "a new spiritual attitude," which he calls "a universal new way of life."[72] The problem of modern culture, Engelmann tells us, it that it is dominated by "hopelessly tangled and confused ideologies," and that what is needed is not another ideology, another dogmatic belief, but a new attitude of "wordless faith" out of which "new forms of society will spring, forms that will need no verbal communication, because they will be lived and thus made manifest. In the future, ideals will not be communicated by attempts to describe them, which inevitably distort, but by the models of an appropriate conduct in life."[73] We might quibble that "faith" is not the best word to use here, implying as it does some form of belief. Indeed, the indeterminate aspects of experience, what Wittgenstein called its ineffable forms which are displayed but cannot be described, require no faith at all; they are as directly experienced, albeit indeterminately, as the appearances or determinate states of affairs which display them. As far as beliefs are concerned, including any held about these ineffable forms, there is literally nothing to say, and no need to say anything.

A life without belief seems to make two things possible: first, liberation from the need to take action based on belief, and second, a peace of mind (ataraxia) born of the freedom from the anxiety induced by the belief in question. The Pyrrhonist continues to act on the basis of appearances; indeed he or she is in a better position to do so than a dogmatist because beliefs held about appearances necessarily substitute for them, and so distort and even deny those appearances. Liberation from belief means no less than liberation from all ideologies and religions. Ours is a culture of belief, one in which the existence and even the necessity of belief is taken for granted. The competition among beliefs is taken as a challenge to sort out "right" beliefs from "wrong" ones. Beliefs are touted as the paths to fulfillment and identity, to the good life; they are said to be the source of values. Given the ungrounded and arbitrary nature of belief, based on one or another nonevident claim, and the proliferation of such claims, it is hardly surprising that this competition of beliefs often turns into a conflict of beliefs. And since there is no way to adjudicate among competing beliefs, violence becomes the ultimate arbiter. If this is so, nonviolence and peace can come about, it seems, only in the absence of belief. This work is intended, in part, to open up that possibility. In world dominated by conflicts among religious and secular beliefs, and marked by conflict and war, unaccountable concentrations of political and economic power, and the destruction of much of the natural environment, it is perhaps high time to explore the prospects of the Pyrrhonist life without beliefs.

In the Buddhist tradition our beliefs are called attachments. We find the following account, among others, of attachment or clinging in an ironically titled Buddhist text, *A Discourse on Right View* in the *Pāli Canon*: "There are these four kinds of clinging: clinging to sensual pleasure, clinging to views, clinging to rules and observances, and clinging to a doctrine of a self."[74] Reading this through the lens of Pyrrhonism, we might say that each of these four is a type of belief, and that belief lies at the basis of attachment. If we cling to the first, sensual pleasure, it is not the pleasure *per se* which motivates us but something we believe *about* that pleasure, namely, that it is somehow essential to our continued existence, that we identify with it, and so on. Views, the second type of clinging, are perhaps closer to what we associate normally with beliefs, that is, the postulating of some kind of nonevident entity of some sort, such as God or the Soul; but again, I must believe something *about* God or the Soul, namely that it exists, displays certain features, and so on. The third type, rules and observances, if they become attachments, might be called rituals; here too some kind of belief in the efficacy of rules and observances, or in their power of manifesting or reenacting some kind of special reality, is required to form an attachment. And finally, the fourth clinging, the notion of the self is perhaps the most widespread and deeply held of all beliefs; most of us presume our own existence as some sort of independently existing entity, one which has a coherent integrity in life and may even survive death. If I cling to any or all of these beliefs, it is because I believe in them, that is, because I postulate them as independently existing entities that somehow command my allegiance, and even my identity. The whole challenge of a life without belief is to suspend judgment about each and all of these, to disavow any allegiance or commitment to them.

One of the principal difficulties for a renewed or revived Pyrrhonism—or for any nondogmatic soteriological practice—is to distinguish belief from knowledge, the nonevident from the evident. In the third chapter we explored the distinction between the evident and the nonevident, and we noted that a recognition of what is evident—our sensations and thoughts—is what distinguishes the Pyrrhonists from other sceptics, who follow the Academic or nihilist tradition. Pyrrhonists recognize appearances and advocate a strict adherence to scientific knowledge of appearances, where hypotheses are subject to empirical tests that confirm or disconfirm them. The difficulty is that often there is no clear line between empirical confirmation and disconfirmation. The stock examples of the Pyrrhonist texts—the body and the soul, smoke and fire—seem transparent enough, but just as often this is not the case. I may have symptoms of a disease, for instance, but not necessarily the disease itself. Or economists may have evidence that the economy is going into recession, but it may not. A trend like global warming may appear, but its scope and duration may remain uncertain. Much of our scientific knowledge is conjectural or statistical, based on evidence that is incomplete or ambiguous. In these domains, of course, the Pyrrhonist would claim no more than to be a seeker, open to further evidence, while living in the meantime with uncertainty, whereas a dogmatist would rush prematurely to a positive or negative conclusion. The hallmark of the Pyrrhonist is restraint, the avoidance of rashness, or any rush to judgment.

Perhaps it is even more difficult to determine beliefs already held or presumed, often unconsciously. "For how does a man learn to recognize his own state of knowing something?"[75] Wittgenstein asks. His answer is to look to empirical evidence, to appearances, to the uses to which we actually put words, to the concrete contexts out of which our language games arise. "An inner experience," he says, "cannot show me that I *know* something."[76] I certainly know that I have the inner experience that I have, say a memory, but I can know, if challenged, that my memory is a memory only if I can also see that it is connected to other experiences beyond itself. I can show my memory is a memory, not a hallucination, only by making such connections. "There is always the danger of wanting to find an expression's meaning by contemplating the expression itself, and the frame of mind in which one uses it, instead of always thinking of the practice."[77] Since we are born into a mostly dogmatic world and learn to play many dogmatic language games, much of what we think we know is really a matter of something we believe rather than know. We learn from our teachers, whose authority we largely accept. Wittgenstein asks: "What kinds of grounds have I for trusting text-books of experimental physics? I have no grounds for not trusting them. And I trust them. I know how such books are produced—or rather, I believe I know. I have some evidence, but it does not go very far and is of a very scattered kind. I have heard, seen and read various things."[78] But this is how we learn what is wrong as well as what is right; it is how we learn beliefs as well as facts. It is how people once learned that the world was flat.

The keenest challenge of Pyrrhonism is to unlearn the beliefs we have incorporated and take for granted, often since childhood, often unconsciously. These beliefs are embedded in language itself, as Wittgenstein made clear, which enables their survival and continued influence. The first step in our liberation from them is the recognition of a certain perplexity they arouse in us, a suspicion that something is puzzling and incoherent about them. Philosophy, as the cliché goes, is said to be born in wonder. Wondering leads to the next step, the active questioning of what we think we know, where the criteria of clarity, if Pyrrhonists are right, can be only the appearances themselves. Appearances are subject to change and dissolution, but they are also enduring and recurring, and above all, unsurpassed in their determinate, involuntary compulsion. The more our beliefs are winnowed out from our appearances, the more our appearances stand forth just as they are, freed of the distortions imposed by our beliefs about them. The more we suspend judgment about beliefs, the more we live in the real world of appearances. The better we understand the determinate nature of our appearances, the better we understand the nature of the indeterminacy that shadows them. Belief falsely tries to make the indeterminate into something determinate; by clarifying what is determinate—what has the specificity of some particular arrangement of parts and wholes—we recognize that there is also something indeterminate. What is indeterminate includes, it seems, our own selves as the subjects of what is determinate (as perceivers of the objects perceived), as well as the forms displayed by what is determinate, what Wittgenstein said could only be *shown*, but not *said*. This questioning brings a kind of enlightenment or understanding, followed, it seems, by the relative peace of mind of *ataraxia*. As Pyrrhonist works from Sextus to Wittgenstein make clear, however, we can expect no comprehensive illumination but only an open-ended series of steps where one suspension of judgment is followed by another. If there is a comprehensive illumination, it is the Buddhists who open us up to it. My effort here will be successful insofar as it contributes, in a small way, to that ongoing process.


## NOTES

1. Stephen Batchelor, *Buddhism Without Beliefs: A Contemporary Guide to Awakening* (New York: Riverhead Books, 1997), 5.
2. Ibid., 37–38.
3. Ibid., 97.
4. Richard H. Popkin, *The History of Scepticism from Erasmus to Descartes*, revised ed. (New York: Harper and Row Torchbook, 1968).
5. Richard H. Popkin, *The High Road to Pyrrhonism*, ed. Richard A. Watson and James E. Force (Indianapolis: Hackett Publishing, 1980).
6. Richard H. Popkin, *The History of Scepticism*, xi.
7. Richard H. Popkin, *The History of Scepticism From Savonarola to Bayle*, revised and expanded edition (Oxford: Oxford University Press, 2003), xix.
8. Ibid., xviii.
9. Ibid., xviii.
10. Ibid., xviii.
11. Ibid., xix.
12. Richard H. Popkin, *The History of Scepticism from Erasmus to Descartes*, 17.
13. Richard H. Popkin, *The History of Scepticism from Savonarola to Bayle*, vi.
14. Ibid., 18.
15. Ibid., 18.
16. Ibid., xxi.
17. Sextus Empiricus, *Outlines of Scepticism* (I, 147), 37–38.
18. Cf. Richard H. Popkin, *The History of Scepticism from Savonarola to Bayle*, 18–27.
19. Ibid., 15.
20. Ibid., 51.
21. Ibid., 173.
22. Sextus Empiricus, *Outlines of Scepticism* (I, 1), 1.
23. Popkin, *The History of Scepticism from Savonarola to Bayle*, 62.
24. See Ibid., 63.
25. Ibid., 173.
26. Ibid., 125.
27. George Berkeley, *A Treatise Concerning the Principles of Human Knowledge*, part I, sec. 3, in *The Works of George Berkeley Bishop of Cloyne*, vol. 2, eds. A. A. Luce and T. E. Jessop (London: Nelson, 1964), 42.
28. George Berkeley, *Three Dialogues Between Hylas and Philonous*, in *The Works of George Berkeley*, vol. 2, 262 (Berkeley's emphasis).

29. Ibid., 167.

30. George Berkeley, *Philosophical Commentaries*, no. 491, in *The Works of George Berkeley*, vol. 1, 61–62.

31. Ibid., no. 658, 80.

32. Ibid., no. 775, 93.

33. Cf. Richard H. Popkin, "Berkeley and Pyrrhonism," in *The High Road to Pyrrhonism*, ed. Richard A. Watson and James E. Force (Indianapolis: Hackett Publishing Co., 1993), 297–318.

34. Cf. Bayle's article "Pyrrho," in Pierre Bayle, *Historical and Critical Dictionary: Selections*, trans. Richard H. Popkin with Craig Brush (Indianapolis: Bobbs-Merrill Company, 1965), 194–209.

35. Popkin, "Berkeley and Pyrrhonism," 25–37.

36. Bayle, "Pyrrho," 194.

37. Ibid., 205.

38. Ibid., 206.

39. See, e.g., Berkeley's works on vision in *The Works of George Berkeley*, vol. 1, including his *Essay Towards a New Theory of Vision* and *Theory of Vision Vindicated*.

40. George Berkeley, *Principles*, sec. 10, *The Works of George Berkeley*, vol. 2, 26.

41. Ibid., sec. 4–5, 23–24.

42. Ibid., Introduction, sec. 18, 16.

43. Cf. Sextus Empiricus, *Outlines of Scepticism* (II, 99–102), 92–93.

44. George Berkeley, Introduction to *Principles*, sec. 16, *The Works of George Berkeley*, vol. 2, 14–15.

45. Ibid., Introduction to *Principles*, sec. 25, 33–34.

46. Ibid., *Principles*, sec. 27, 52.

47. George Berkeley, "On the Will of God," *The Works of George Berkeley*, vol. 7, 130.

48. George Berkeley, "On the Mission of Christ," Ibid., 41.

49. George Berkeley, "On the Will of God," Ibid., 131.

50. George Berkeley, *Principles*, sec. 3, *The Works of George Berkeley*, vol. 2, 42.

51. George Berkeley, *Principles*, sec. 29, Ibid, 53.

52. George Berkeley, *Principles*, sec. 30, Ibid., 53.

53. At least not one he wrote about. He may have in fact developed some kind of meditative technique. He spent three years in Rhode Island in colonial America (1729–1731), where he built a house that is now a landmark administered by the International Berkeley Society. As a visitor, I was told that Berkeley was known to have spent much time sitting alone on a nearby local landmark, a vast rock formation overlooking the ocean, deep in contemplation.

54. David Hume, *An Enquiry Concerning Human Understanding*, ed. Eric Steinberg (Indianapolis: Hackett Publishing, 1993), 107 (Hume's emphasis).

55. "[T]he reason why I give no sources is that it is a matter of indifference to me whether the thoughts that I have had have been anticipated by somebody else." Ludwig Wittgenstein, Authors' Preface, *Tractatus Logico-Philosophicus*,

trans. D. F. Pears and B. F. McGuinness (London: Routledge and Kegan Paul, 1961), 3; cf. Paul Englemann, *Letters from Ludwig Wittgenstein with a Memoir* (New York: Horizon Press, 1967), 106–7: "whenever he [Wittgenstein] did read such [philosophical] literature, he found that it had little or nothing to give him. Therefore he did not feel any obligation whatever to scan those books in order to ascertain whether their ideas agreed or conflicted with his own."

56. Ludwig Wittgenstein, *Tractatus*, 3.

57. Ibid., 7.

58. "[A] certain colour, taste, smell, figure and consistence having been observed to go together, are accounted one distinct thing, signified by the name *apple*. Other collections of ideas constitute a stone, a tree, a book, and the like sensible things; which, as they are pleasing or disagreeable, excite the passions of love, hatred, joy, grief, and so forth." George Berkeley, *Principles*, sec. 1, in *Works of George Berkeley*, vol. 2, 42.

59. Ludwig Wittgenstein, *On Certainty*, trans. Denis Paul and G. E. M. Anscombe (New York: Harper Torchbooks, 1969), 18.

60. Ibid., 22.

61. Ibid., 40.

62. Ibid., 44.

63. Ibid., 59.

64. Ludwig Wittgenstein, *Tractatus*, 149.

65. Ibid., 23.

66. Ibid., 51.

67. Paul Engelmann, *Letters from Ludwig Wittgenstein*, 101–2.

68. Sextus Empiricus, *Outlines of Scepticism* (I, vii), 6.

69. Ludwig Wittgenstein, *Tractatus*, 49.

70. I have developed this "logic" of representation and contrast elsewhere; cf. Adrian Kuzminski, *The Soul* (New York: Peter Lang, 1994), 21–42.

71. Quoted by Allan Janik and Stephen Toulmin in *Wittgenstein's Vienna* (New York: Simon & Schuster, 1973), 192, emphases by Wittgenstein; cf. the passage quoted earlier by Stephen Batchelor in regard to Buddhism where he says that "experience . . . is simultaneously knowable and unknowable." Stephen Batchelor, *Buddhism Without Beliefs*, 97; I have also written about this aspect of Wittgenstein's thought; cf. Adrian Kuzminski, "Wittgenstein's Mystical Realism," *The Yale Review*, Summer 1979, 500–518.

72. Paul Engelmann, *Letters from Wittgenstein*, 135.

73. Ibid., 135.

74. *In the Buddha's Words: An Anthology of Discourses from the Pāli Canon*, ed. Bhikkhu Bodhi (Boston: Wisdom Publications, 2005), 328–29.

75. Ludwig Wittgenstein, *On Certainty*, 77.

76. Ibid., 75.

77. Ibid., 79.

78. Ibid., 79.

# Bibliography

*Ancilla to The Pre-Socratic Philosophers.* Kathleen Freeman, trans. Cambridge, Mass.: Harvard University Press, 1966.

Aristotle. *Metaphysics.* Richard Hope, trans. Ann Arbor: Ann Arbor Paperbacks, University of Michigan Press, 1960.

Batchelor, Stephen. *Buddhism Without Beliefs: A Contemporary Guide to Awakening.* New York: Riverhead Books, 1997.

Bayle, Pierre. *Historical and Critical Dictionary: Selections.* Richard H. Popkin and Craig Brush, trans. Indianapolis: Bobbs-Merrill Company, 1965.

Berkeley, George. *A Treatise Concerning the Principles of Human Knowledge,* Part I. In *Principles, Dialogues, and Philosophical Correspondence.* Colin Murray Turbayne, ed. New York: Bobbs-Merrill, 1965.

———. *The Works of George Berkeley, Bishop of Cloyne.* 9 vols. A. A. Luce and T. E. Jessop, eds. London: Nelson, 1964.

Bett, Richard. *Pyrrho: His Antecedents, and His Legacy.* Oxford: Oxford University Press, 2000.

Buddhaghosa, Bhadantācariya. *The Path of Purification [Visuddhimagga].* Bhikkhu Nanamoli, trans. Kandy, Sri Lanka: Buddhist Publication Society, 1991.

Burnyeat, M. F. "Can the Sceptic Live his Scepticism?" In *Doubt and Dogmaticism: Studies in Hellenistic Epistemology.* Malcolm Schofield, Myles Burnyeat, and Jonathan Barnes, eds. Oxford: Clarendon Press, 1980.

Burton, David. *Emptiness Appraised: A Critical Study of Nāgārjuna's Philosophy.* Delhi: Motilal Banarsidass, 1999.

Candrakīrti. *Madhyamakāvatāra [The Entry into the Middle Way].* In *The Emptiness of Emptiness: An Introduction to Early Indian Mādhyamika.* C. W. Huntington, Jr., and Geshe Namgyai Wangchen, trans. and commentary. Honolulu: University of Hawaii Press, 1989.

Carpenter, Rhys. *Beyond the Pillars of Heracles: The Classical World seen Through the Eyes of Its Discoverers.* New York: Delacourt, 1966.

Casson, Lionel. *Libraries in the Ancient World*. New Haven, Conn.: Yale University Press, 2001.

Cicero. *Academica*. H. Rackham, trans. Loeb Classical Library. Cambridge, Mass.: Harvard University Press, 1961.

Coupris, Dirk, Robert Han, and Gerard Naddaf. *Anaximander in Context: New Studies in the Origins of Greek Philosophy*. Albany: State University Press of New York, 2003.

Diogenes Laertius. *Lives of the Eminent Philosophers*. 2 vols. R. D. Hicks, trans. Loeb Classical Library. Cambridge, Mass.: Harvard University Press, 2000.

Engelmann, Paul. *Letters from Ludwig Wittgenstein with a Memoir*. New York: Horizon Press, 1967.

Flintoff, Everard. "Pyrrho and India." *Phronesis* XXV, No. 2, 1980.

Fox, Warwick. "Arne Naess: A Biographical Sketch." http://trumpeter .athabascau.ca/content/v9.2/fox.html, accessed October 2005.

Gomez, Luis. O. "Proto-Madhyamaka in the Pāli Canon." In *Philosophy East and West* 26, no. 2, April 1976.

Hamilton, Sue. *Early Buddhism: A New Approach: The I of the Beholder*. Richmond, Surrey: Curzon, 2000.

Hankinson. R. J. *The Sceptics*. New York: Routledge, 1995. http://trumpeter .athabascau.ca/content/v9.2/fox.html, accessed October 2005.

*The Hellenistic Philosophers*. 2 vols. A. A. Long and D. N. Sedley, trans. and eds. Cambridge: Cambridge University Press, 1987.

Herodotus. *The History*. David Grene, trans. Chicago: University of Chicago Press, 1987.

"Hesychast." *Catholic Encyclopedia*. www.newadvent.org/cathen/07301a.thm, accessed February 2004.

*The Holy Teaching of Vimalakirti*. Robert A. F. Thurman, trans. University Park: Pennsylvania State University Press, 1976.

Hume, David. *An Inquiry Concerning Human Understanding*, second ed. Eric Steinberg, ed. Indianapolis: Hackett Publishing, 1993.

Huntington, C. W., Jr. "Was Candrakīrti a Prāsaṅgika?" In *The Svātantrika-Prā saṅgika Distinction: What Difference does a Difference Make?* Georges J. J. Dreyfus and Sara L. McClintock, eds. Boston: Wisdom Publications, 2003.

*In the Buddha's Words: An Anthology of Discourses from the Pāli Canon*. Bhikkhu Bodhi, ed. Boston: Wisdom Publications, 2005.

"India," in *The Oxford Classical Dictionary*, N. G. L. Hammond and H. H. Scullard, eds. Oxford: Clarendon Press, 1970.

Jain, Hiralal. *Jainism in Buddhist Literature*. www.ibiblio.org/jainism/database/ BOOK/jainbudh.doc, accessed February 2004.

Janik, Allan, and Stephen Toulmin. *Wittgenstein's Vienna*. New York: Simon & Schuster, 1973.

Kant, Immanuel. *Critique of Pure Reason*. Norman Kempt Smith, trans. New York: St. Martin's Press, 1965.

Kuzminski, Adrian. *The Soul*. New York: Peter Lang Publishing, 1994.

——. "Wittgenstein's Mystical Realism." In *The Yale Review*, Summer 1979.

*The Long Discourses of the Buddha [Digha Nikaya]*. Maurice Walshe, trans. Boston: Wisdom Publications, 1995.

Long, Herbert S. "Introduction." Diogenes Laertius. *Lives of Eminent Philosophers*. Vol. 1. R. D. Hicks, trans. Loeb Classical Library. Cambridge, Mass.: Harvard University Press, 2000.

McEvilley, Thomas. "Pyrrhonism and Madhyamaka." In *Philosophy East and West* 32, no. 1, January 1982.

———. *The Shape of Ancient Thought: Comparative Studies in Greek and Indian Philosophies*. New York: Allworth Press, 2002.

"Megasthenes." *The Oxford Classical Dictionary*. N. G. L. Hammond and H. H. Schullard, eds. Oxford: Clarendon Press, 1970,

*The Middle Length Discourses of the Buddha [Majjhima Nikaya]*. Bhikkhu Nanamoli, trans. Bhikkhu Bodhi, ed. Boston: Wisdom Publications, 1995.

Naess, Arne. *Scepticism*. London: Routledge & Kegan Paul, 1968.

Nagao, Gadjin M. *Madhyamaka and Yogācāra*. Albany: State University of New York Press, 1991.

Nāgārjuna. *Mūlamadhyamakakārikā [The Fundamental Wisdom of the Middle Way]*. Jay L. Garfield, trans. and commentary. In *The Fundamental Wisdom of the Middle Way: Nāgārjuna's Mūlamadhyamikakārikā*. New York and Oxford: Oxford University Press, 1995.

Nietzsche, Friedrich. *The Will to Power*. Walter Kaufmann and R. J. Hollingdale, trans. New York: Vintage Books, 1968.

Nussbaum, Martha C. *The Therapy of Desire: Theory and Practice in Hellenistic Ethics*. Princeton, N.J.: Princeton University Press, 1994.

*The Original Sceptics: A Controversy*. Myles Burnyeat and Michael Frede, eds. Indianapolis: Hackett Publishing Company, 1997.

*The Perfection of Wisdom in Eight Thousand Lines and Its Verse Summary*. Edward Conze, trans. San Francisco: City Lights, 2006.

Plutarch. *The Lives of the Noble Grecians and Romans*. John Dryden, trans. Arthur Hugh Clough, rev. trans. New York: Modern Library, n.d.

Popkin, Richard H. *The High Road to Pyrrhonism*. Richard A. Watson and James E. Force, eds. Indianapolis: Hackett Publishing Company, 1980.

———. *The History of Scepticism from Erasmus to Descartes*, rev. ed. New York: Harper and Row Torchbook, 1968.

———. *The History of Scepticism from Savonarola to Bayle*, rev. ed. Oxford: Oxford University Press, 2003.

Porphry. "On the Life of Plotinus and the Arrangement of his Works." In *Plotinus. The Enneads*. Stephen MacKenna, trans. London: Penguin Books, 1991.

Possehl, Gregory L. *The Indus Civilization: A Contemporary Perspective*. Walnut Creek, Calif.: Altamira Press, 2002.

Priestley, C. D. C. *Pudgalavada Buddhism: The Reality of the Indeterminate Self*. Toronto: University of Toronto, Center for South Asian Studies, 1999.

Samkara. *The Thousand Teachings [Upadesa Sahasri]*. A. J. Alston, trans. London: Shanti Sadan, 1990.

Senden, M. von. *Space and Sight: The Perception of Space and Shape in the Congenitally Blind Before and After Operation*. Peter Heath, trans. Glencoe, Ill.: The Free Press, 1960.

Sextus Empiricus. *Outlines of Pyrrhonism*. R. G. Bury, trans. Loeb Classical Library. Cambridge, Mass.: Harvard University Press, 2000.

——. *Against the Logicians*. R. G. Bury, trans. Loeb Classical Library. Cambridge, Mass.: Harvard University Press, 1997.

——. *Against the Physicists. Against the Ethicists*. R. G. Bury, trans. Cambridge, Mass.: Cambridge University Press, 1997.

——. *Against the Professors*. R. G. Bury, trans. Cambridge, Mass.: Cambridge University Press, 2000.

——. *Outlines of Scepticism*. Julia Annas and Jonathan Barnes, trans. Cambridge: Cambridge University Press, 2000.

Strabo. *Geography*. Horace Leonard Jones, trans. Loeb Classical Library. Cambridge, Mass: Harvard University Press, 1966.

*Sutta Nipāta*. H. Saddhastissa, trans. London: Curzon Press, 1985.

Thorsrud, Harald. "Ancient Greek Scepticism." *The Internet Encyclopaedia of Philosophy*. www.utm.edu/research/iep/s/skepanci.htlm, accessed June 2003.

Upatissa, Arahant. *The Path of Freedom [Vimutimmagga]*. N. R. M. Ehara, Soma Thera, and Sheminda Thera, trans. Kandy, Sri Lanka: Buddhist Publication Society, 1995.

Vassiliades, Demetrois. Th. *The Greeks in India: A Survey in Philosophical Understanding*. New Dehli: Munshiram Manoharlal Publishers Pvt. Ltd., 2000.

Warren, James. *Epicurus and Democritean Ethics: An Archaeology of Ataraxia*. Cambridge: Cambridge University Press, 2002.

Wittgenstein, Ludwig. *On Certainty*. G. E. M. Anscombe and G. H. con Wright, trans. New York: Harper and Row, 1972.

——. *Tractatus Logico-Philosophicus*. D. F. Pears and B. F. McGuinness, trans. London: Routledge and Kegan Paul, 1961.

# Index

# About the Author

**Adrian Kuzminski** lives in rural upstate New York. He has been resident scholar in philosophy at Hartwick College since 1997. Previously he was a professor of history at the University of Hawaii. He is the author of *The Soul*, published in 1994, and of the forthcoming *Fixing the System: A History Of Populism, Ancient and Modern.*